Hack The Buyer Brain

KENDA MACDONALD

Hack
The
Buyer Brain

A revolutionary approach to sales, marketing, and creating a profitable customer journey

First edition published 2019
© Kenda Macdonald

Published by
www.elitepublishingacademy.com

Printed and bound in Great Britain by
www.elitepublishingacademy.com

A catalogue record for this book
is available from The British Library
ISBN
978-1-912713-95-0

To the women in my life.

The women in my past that shaped my present.

The women in my present that create my future.

*And the women of the future that will
learn from the past and present.*

*Each and every one of you are worth celebrating,
for together we hold the power of change.*

Let's hack today for a better tomorrow.

Founding Hackers

Debbie Ekins

Kathleen Elliott

James Steel

Emma Wilberforce

Tom Wardman

Tim Wilson-Frier

Catherine Spencer-Smith

Jackie Johnson

Emma Stewart

Lyndsay Cambridge

Martin Huntbach

Cara Marshall

Imogen Allen

Sally Comfort

Sallie Golding

Matt Davies

Ross Coverdale

Elena Panarese

Darren Moore

Suzanne Bird

Sally Tudhope

Emily Wyman

Sarah Mulcare

Jillian Littlejohn

Olayinka Ewuola

Natalie Luckham

Craig Pugsley

Ahmed Khalifa

Cathy Wassell

John Espirian

Edd Hurst

Karen Aston

Michael Gearon

Julia Brown

Michael Thomas

David Artiss

Andrew and Pete

Clare Murthy

Nancy Seeger

Michelle Osorio-Martin

Sarah Laws

Daniel Runarsson

Arfa Saira Iqbal

ReddyVar Katzy

David Withington

Emma Wood

Russ Haworth

Ramin Nakisa

Evangelos Magoulas

Sarah Watz

Beka Ventham

Amy Kate Walden

K M Cusack

Jules Spencer-Smith

Somi Arian

Alison Boyle

Emily Buehler

Kris Allen

Emily Chung
Julia Bramble
Candice Stapper
Donna Beckett
Harjit Sohotey-Khan
Ilka Salzmann
Abi Hall
Oskar Barczak
Fiona Honeyman
Catie Holdridge
Samantha McGowan
Danielle Ebbage
Lauren Fowles
Bradley Mursell
Emily Hopkins
Rebecca Stonehouse
Elaine Madden
Rae Boyle
Megan Atkins
Nobu Tanaka
Martin Van Dam
Sam Bauyumi
Lisa Cooper
Matthew Barr
Elena Berrino
Paul Crowley
Graham Cullis
Simon Fletcher
J M Lecchini
Laura Robinson
Colleen Kochannek

Jason Kruger
Jeremy Crudup
Vicki La Bouchardiere
Pam Seran
Gregory Jenkins
Paul Tansey
Alex Lowe
Lucy Barfoot
Andrew Hawkins
Col Gray
Chris Marr
Krista Bakker
Vicky Fraser
Ian McConnachie
Tanya Smith
Neil Bayley-Hay
Nick Wilsdon
George Fox
Andrew McEwan
Ana Garrancho
Caitlyn Foster
Heidi Strickland-Clark
Austen Clark
Elba Nino
Sandra Palmer-Snellin,
Yva Yorston
Richard Winfield
David Drimmie
Nicola Crawford
Marissa Waite

Paul Tansey, Director/Founder, Intergage

I'm a fifty-something marketing sales and marketing veteran. I am a managing director and a speaker, a marketing nerd—and a big fan of Kenda Macdonald. *Hack The Buyer Brain* (HTBB) is a journey into the mind of an expert in marketing automation, and as such it's not a journey I wanted to miss. I'm proud to call Kenda a friend. She's completely obsessed by the psychology of selling and, I swear, she thinks of little else most of the time.

Kenda is an accomplished speaker and an award-winning business woman... and I was being given the opportunity to download some of her precious, hard-earned knowledge. It was an opportunity I couldn't miss. I jumped on board that train just as soon as it pulled into the station.

I felt privileged. One rainy Saturday I sat down with a coffee, a manuscript of what would become *Hack the Buyer Brain,* and a mind-mapping app to document what I thought were her key findings. Several hours and 10 coffees later, I had a huge mind map and I had changed... I was excited... I was a better marketer.

So what's the book like and who is it for?

It's for all of us trying to get our heads around the complexities of marketing and sales in the digital world. We are all designing customer experiences—and these experiences have to go well beyond the purchase. *Hack the Buyer Brain* provides a framework and a set of rules any marketer can follow. Since reading it, I have referred back to it often.

I study this stuff all the time but I found the *HTBB* experience educational, authoritative, well-researched, and logical. Above all, though, it was compelling and I wanted to keep reading it. I read only really good books in one go. I refer back only to exceptional ones such as this. Read it now to become a better marketer.

George Fox, CEO

Hack The Buyer Brain combines the latest revelations in behavioural science with immediately applicable marketing strategies and tactics. In my opinion, this is the most practical and helpful book in the buyer psychology and marketing subgenre.

Kenda consistently unpacks consumer psychology and the stages of the buying process in an eloquent, accessible and enjoyable way. Perhaps the biggest takeaway from this book crammed-full of hidden gems is the attention Kenda pays to the consideration phase that consumers go through.

Not all purchases are created equal. Low-expense, low-stakes purchases have the shortest consideration stage, whereas high-expense, high-stakes purchases may warrant lengthy consideration. And that's okay. Kenda argues that marketers should focus on behavioural selling and tracking engagement. Collectively, marketers should welcome and respect the need for consumers to research and consider purchases.

For too long, people have felt disconnected and deceived by salespeople. The lack of trust has led to research-obsessed consumers that want to be helped in their problem-solving, not sold to. *Hack The Buyer Brain* welcomes the shift to consumer power, and tells marketers not to fear. Kenda's lifecycle marketing plan redefined how I thought about marketing. As I continued through each chapter that carefully walks through each steps including the psychological context, marketing frameworks and case studies, I realised that embracing the buyer process and not attempting to constrain it, would be a path to business success.

By the end of this book, I nearly had a notepad full of notes that I started implementing the next day. In a subgenre that has too often showed marketers a lot, but only told us a little, Kenda breaks the mould. A must read for those striving to be a complete marketer.

Vicky Fraser, Moxie Books

I've had the privilege of helping Kenda put the finishing touches to *Hack The Buyer Brain*—and it's been an absolute delight.

When you find yourself breaking off from your task to scribble excited notes to yourself, you know you're onto a good thing.

Kenda first told me she was writing a book in the summer of 2018 and—because books is what I do—I was naturally excited. But more than that, I knew the business world was crying out for a book that really digs into buyer psychology.

Most of us don't really think much about why we do the things we do, how our brains work, and the problems this causes us as business owners and marketers. Kenda does. She's incredibly nerdy about it and I love her for that.

HTBB is a full-on exploration of how our brains work, why business owners should care, and how to use these psychological insights to sell.

But more importantly—at least, I think it's more important—this book helps business owners put the client first. I've a background in direct response marketing, so I've known for a long time that the most successful businesses aren't just about making cold, hard cash. I've always wanted to market my business in such a way that I help make the world a better place. But books explaining precisely how to do that are few and far between.

You don't make headlines and win clickbait contests by being warm and fuzzy; you do it by promising to 10X results and hustle and smash it and make a bazillion quid in a weekend.

Kenda lifts the lid on that shite and shows us how to make more money ethically, how to improve people's lives and—yes—how to increase profits in a steady and sustainable way.

If you want to change lives *and* sell more stuff, read this book. Then read it again. Then *take action on it.*

Contents

On Survival

It's amazing how resourceful we can be when our survival is threatened.

I happen to be excellent at what I do—I build fantastic and robust marketing automation campaigns in Infusionsoft by Keap, a top-of-the-line marketing automation platform. It's easy to be good at something when it's fun: the idea of combining behaviour and marketing fascinates me, and I know it makes for better-converting campaigns.

I learned this skill to pay my way through university, where I was studying for a degree in forensic psychology. I'd been trying to get my boss to look at the behavioural aspect of sales because I could see a pattern in the problems lots of our clients were facing: they weren't accounting for how humans behave when they designed their marketing strategies. I was still struggling to get him on board with this concept when he told me it was all over and he was closing down the business.

I'd built a team in my former boss's company, and they had just hired my fiancé. We were moving to a new home to be closer to the business. In fact, it was moving day when he dropped his news and we were still unpacking the trucks.

1

We were also planning a wedding and had already committed to the date and venue.

And then there were my university fees. Oh, God! My university fees. So when my former boss told me he'd run the company into the ground while we were uprooting our lives to support it, with all this running through my head I think I was too panicked to cry. Mike and I had no jobs now—what the hell was I going to do? I took Mike outside and said, 'We don't have jobs. I think we should start a company.'

And so we did.

Automation Ninjas was born in 2014, in a state of determination and barely controlled terror. 2015 was rough. Really rough. I had less than six months left of a four-year slog through university. Getting my degree, then my masters, then my PhD, was all I ever wanted to do. But there was no financial help available to me as an international student—I either paid up or dropped out.

I dropped out.

My identity was so tied up in my education that I floundered for a while. But then I started to research buyer psychology obsessively, blending it with what I was already good at: marketing automation.

To my absolute delight, the results were spectacular. I haven't looked back since.

At Automation Ninjas we focus on combining my understanding of buyer psychology with marketing automation, to build marketing strategies that engage and convert.

This book takes what I've learned, and the strategies and stories our clients are enjoying, and makes it accessible to the business community at large. I hope you enjoy what's in the pages to come, and I hope you learn and implement as you go along.

If you're in a tough place right now, I've been there and I know what it's like. I hope using this book brings you the success you're striving for.

—Kenda

INTRODUCTION: Before We Get Started

Before we get rolling, let's get on the same page. I don't want to waste your time, so before we get into the good stuff let's make sure you're in the right place. This book is for you if:

You care about your customers

If you want to improve your marketing strategy and give your customers the best possible experience, read on.

You recognise the need for change

If you understand you need to find a marketing strategy you can pick up and adapt to suit your specific needs, this book is for you. But first a warning—if you only take little bits away and don't apply the whole process, this won't work. This strategy is bigger than the sum of its parts. The beauty is in how they work together as a system.

You know there's no such thing as a magic bullet

Implementing the strategy outlined in this book takes effort and hard work. All good stuff does. While there are some things you'll be able to fix faster than others, it's won't happen overnight. If you're looking for a quick fix you won't find it here.

You're prepared for some hard work

As I said, understanding and implementing this strategy does need work. If you don't want to put in any effort, success is not going to happen. Running a successful business takes effort. If you want to thrive in a future which will be all about personalised consumer experience, put some elbow grease in.

You're looking for science-based evidence and real-life examples

This book is based on concepts some of the best marketers of all time have been using for decades—but they didn't know *why* what they were doing worked. We now have the evidence-based knowledge they didn't, which makes our lives that little bit easier.

Every chapter is validated, not only with real-life examples but with science, too. I've included the science because I need hard evidence, not just anecdotes, to be convinced something works. If I'm making claims about something to you, I want you to be confident that what I'm sharing works.

Time is a precious resource that should not be squandered, so if this book isn't right for you, I won't be offended if you put it down. If you're still here, welcome! I hope you'll relish the insights in the coming pages. Time for the good stuff now...

Why I've Written This Book

My mission is to make buyer psychology accessible to business owners just like you, so you can combine those psychology insights with your marketing and automation strategies.

I want to show you the framework in which you can build highly engaged, meaningful connections with your customers, making them happy and putting more money in your bank account. I'd like to fill the internet with more value and less noise by helping you be targeted about what you do.

Together we'll explore the framework combining behaviour, automated lifecycle marketing, and content. I'll uncover the *why* and empower you with the *how*, and together we'll unlock your behavioural journey strategy so you have the tools you need to bridge the consumer–business divide.

The State We're In

First, though: how did we get here? Business has undergone a massive shift since the 1980s, particularly since 1995. In 1980, the pioneers of the digital world released the first home computers. Although the '1977 trinity' of computers (the Commodore PET, the Apple II, and the TRS-80) had changed the way people worked, it was only when computers entered our homes that things started to really move and shake.

The 80s and 90s saw huge cultural changes: advances in technology made the world that little bit smaller and hugely more enlightened, and in 1982 *Time* magazine named 'the computer' as machine of the year. In 1989 Sir Tim Berners-Lee proposed creating the World Wide Web and by 1995 the world was a radically different place, with almost 40 million people using the new internet.

At the time of writing there are over 3.2 billion people online. That's more than half the global population. Facebook alone is now more than 50 times bigger than the whole of the internet was in 1995[1].

The internet has changed everything, and the access we now have to information has changed what we do and how we do it. Before the internet came along, you could tell a consumer anything you wanted and they would probably believe you. Even in the early days of the internet, businesses still had the upper hand. Sales people were in charge—they commanded the price, the service, and the goods because they controlled the information. To buy anything, you went through some form of sales process: you were told what you wanted to know and then you'd get what you wanted.

With the dawning of the internet age, people began to put information online—and others with computers in their homes or libraries half a world away could see that information. Suddenly, the world shrank and exploded all at the same time—and the control started slipping.

Power Shift

As control of the sales process slipped from the hands of businesses, it landed firmly in the lap of consumers. Today, we have more information

---

1 'The rather petite internet of 1995' Pingdom https://royal.pingdom.com/2011/03/31/internet-1995/

than we know what to do with. Everyone and their grandmother (mine included, who rocks her smartphone) has searched online: we all know what to do to get the information we desire. We have all the information we need at our fingertips, whenever we want to access it.

In the last five years there has also been a revolution in how we access this information. Smartphones, tablets, and laptops mean we have access to information on the go. We can consume that information via text, video, or audio. Businesses that still try to play the 'I have the power' game are not fighting a losing battle—they're fighting a battle that was lost long ago.

On top of this, consumers don't just want all the information, they want it on their own terms. They want to consume what they want, how they want, when they want. While there are hundreds of different types of consumers, the one thing they all have in common is they do not like being sold to—unless it fits their agenda.

If the sales process is part of what they want, they will grin and bear it. But if the sales process interrupts what they're doing uninvited, be prepared to face the wrath of a disgruntled customer with an internet connection and access to the world.

Consumers are wising up to interruption sales. Ad blockers mean we can all switch off interruptions completely. Your customers will flock to services where they don't have to watch adverts and can consume at their own pace—like Netflix. Personalised and tailored services are becoming the norm: Facebook, YouTube, Netflix, and your local supermarket all tailor content. Consumers want what they want—nothing more and nothing less.

Keeping Up

Businesses, on the other hand, need to cut through the noise of the internet. They need to get in front of as many people as possible, so they flock to places where consumers spend their time, then spend money trying to get their foot in the door—often with mixed results.

Most customers hate this type of marketing, but when they really need something they'll engage with it; they'll go in with their guard up and click around to find out what they need to know. The problem here is it's getting harder and harder to interrupt the consumer. And because it's getting harder, it's also getting more expensive.

Welcome to our big problem: businesses need customers, but now consumers will come to you only when they're ready, and not before. This divide between what businesses need and what consumers want is growing constantly. We need to find a way to bridge that gap before we get lost in the chasm in the middle.

Technology is moving at a crazy pace to try to resolve this. More and more software or advertising tricks and tactics pop up every day, purporting to solve all our problems. And some of it does. Some of it is genuinely amazing.

But one kink in the system is that it's also quite overwhelming. There are far more shiny new things coming out than the average business can keep up with. For some businesses, this is exciting and thrilling (I know I fall into that category). For others, though, it's frustrating and bewildering. For all of us there's an element of running to stand still— we're barely keeping our heads above the deluge.

The other kink is many of these shiny new solutions focus on tactics, not fixing the overall problem. We're not dipping our toes into the pool of the Information Age anymore; the Information Age has grown up into a big angry sea and we're waist deep in it. Soon we won't be able to stand. Both businesses and consumers need a life raft now, or at the very least a flotation device to cling to until things calm down a little.

As this business–consumer relationship keeps changing, so does the role of marketing. Marketing always used to be the colouring-in club in the corner of the office where people with weird fashion taste made pretty things that sounded nice. But marketing has become so much more than that.

Marketing doesn't just funnel leads into sales anymore. It gets the leads, it educates the leads, it passes them to sales to take the money, then it takes them back so the business can retain the customer. Marketing is now everything we do to get and keep a customer. Because of that, marketing automation isn't just email campaigns—it's a mind-boggling range of tech to help you do everything you need to get and keep a customer.

Since I started Automation Ninjas in 2014, I've seen hundreds of businesses struggle with these changing roles. It's hard enough to adapt to and cope with all these changes in marketing; add the shift in consumer behaviour, and it's even tougher.

Cracking The Code

The behaviour consumers display can be bewildering to the uninitiated. It seems like customers are ever-changing and never pleased. The speed at which the internet enables this change feels frantic and fraught, and many businesses simply aren't keeping their heads above water.

With my background in forensic psychology, I've been watching these changes with keen interest. When you have a little know-how, you understand there are reasons why consumers do what they do: there are patterns, and consumers leave unmistakable behavioural traces behind. Consumers' behaviour tells us what they want—but most of us don't have the skills to crack their code. That code is behaviour.

I started Automation Ninjas to help business owners leverage behaviour in their marketing. As marketing shifts and consumers demand more from businesses, the odd quirks of the human condition increasingly affect how we buy, sell, and conduct ourselves. For years, I've seen businesses struggle with marketing strategies that simply don't take behaviour into consideration. It's a fundamental flaw in current marketing. To bridge the divide between what consumers want and what businesses need, we must combine understanding and strategy and integrate buyer psychology into marketing.

Once we understand *why* consumers do what they do, we can create marketing that works. We can focus on finding better customers and work towards higher return on investment from far more ethical advertising. We can build trust. And we can waste less time and money.

Ultimately, you want a happy consumer who spends more money, more often. That kind of repeat business is known as customer lifetime value, and it's gold dust. To get to the point where customers keep coming back for more, we need to understand human behaviour and human needs. And we need to understand the brain. The long and short of it is, the brain is full of problems when it comes to selling. We evolved to survive, not to buy. Modern life causes us to use parts of our brain for things they were never intended to be used for. All day, every day, we hack our own brains to get around this issue. Fortunately those hacks are now scientifically observed and predictable.

Get clarity on how that hacking works, and you can hack the hacking—increasing your profits and outrunning your competition. So let's get started!

How To Read This Book

To make this as easy as possible, while being as thorough as possible, each chapter is structured into four sections:

1. *The Principle*

We start each chapter with the main concept. This tells you the background you need to know and explains the premise.

2. *Real Life*

The second part is a real-life story and case study showing the principle being used so you can see how it works in real life and get some perspective. To keep this nice and unbiased I've made sure not to just put our own clients in there. These strategies are being used successfully all over the world by many different businesses—you'll see proof of that.

3. *The Science*

The third part is the science or data behind the idea. This will give you a depth of understanding of the concept that most books won't give you. I've included this so it's easier for you to execute the idea properly. It's also just really, really cool!

4. *The Hacks*

The fourth part of each chapter is a summary of what we've covered. You'll see what the brain is hacking, and how you can hack the hack.

You need a foundational understanding of behaviour first—so that's how I've structured the book. Next, we'll walk through the behavioural framework. Then we'll dig into content, and finally you'll get a structure you can take away and use immediately in your own marketing.

My hope is this book will change the way you engage with your customers for the better. I can't wait to see how you take this information and apply it to your business—so please get in touch and let me know how you get on. And now, it's time to get started now—so let's dive straight into behaviour and look at how the brain actually works.

CHAPTER 1: Behaviour—Where The Hacking Begins

"Experience is the child of Thought, and Thought is the child of Action."

~ Benjamin Disreli

CHAPTER 1: Behaviour—Where The Hacking Begins

Behaviour: The Principle & The Problem

What makes people buy a Land Rover Defender over the world's most beautiful car, the Jaguar E-Type? It's vital to understand the reason consumers will choose one over the other.

For those not in the know, Enzo Ferrari proclaimed the Jaguar E-Type to be the 'most beautiful car in the world' when it was released in March 1961. I don't think it's the most beautiful car in the world. Sorry Enzo! And while I'm probably a heathen and certainly not much of a car person, I am very much in love with the Land Rover Defender—and I'm not alone.

More than two million of the beasts were made over 68 years, and they are the most iconic all-terrain vehicles out there. When production stopped in 2016 there was public outcry—people were furious. When the replacement was revealed, the motoring public was so upset the plans were scrapped. Since then, secret developments have been happening. Land Rover won't reveal much about the new Defender until it's released. The question is, why are people so emotionally invested in the Defender? And what makes it, and the E-Type, so iconic?

The answer lies in driver experience. Breaking it down to absolute basics, both cars will get you from A to B. In that respect, they're the same: a mode of transport.

Going deeper, the first difference is in *how* they get you there. One gets you there fast and makes you feel like a superstar while doing it; the other gets you there no matter what's in the way and you'll feel invincible while doing it.

Each car oozes experience. E-Types are sleek, smooth and iconic, and they're seductive by nature—you feel that when you sit inside one.

Defenders, on the other hand, scream utility. Their chunky, boxy shape tells you they're made for working and playing hard. They often have winches, snorkels, and spades bolted onto the front. Look at a Defender and you know it can do anything, anywhere. They make no apologies for being beautiful brutes.

The key to both these icons is they were designed for the experience. *Not the other way around.* Each component is made to fit with what each car is designed to do. Every little touch is there because it adds to the overall experience. They exude their experience because that's what they were created to do, and the experience is what fans are drawn to— or we'd all be driving the same car. Taking away that experience makes everyone really unhappy, as Land Rover quickly discovered.

Experience is everything. That's been true since those cars went to market and it's true now more than ever. A report from Walker Research says by 2020 experience will be the number one decider for consumers, more than either price or quality[1]. That means your consumers will judge you based purely on what the overall experience is like. Which begs the question—can you currently provide a good enough experience from start to finish in order to make that difference? If not, you have work to do.

I believe we've already reached the point Walker Research refers to. The second a consumer has the means to afford an experience they will pay for it, whether it's spending more on a fancy car, a fancy house or a fancy television. We pay for experience if the product matters to us. The experience used to be a luxury or privilege, but that's changing. Experience is now often the deciding factor.

---

1 'Customers: The future of B-to-B customer experience' (2013) Walker Research

As a consumer, the changes businesses are being forced to make because of our demands are exciting. The entire buying process is constantly being innovated and improved on, and it's lovely to live through. Consumption is becoming easier, smoother and more pleasant all the time. But as a business, what you need to provide for an ever-more discerning consumer base can be intimidating.

If consumers are demanding a certain level of experience, how do you then ensure you nail the experience before it's too late? First, you need to design for it. The problem we have today is businesses create products, decide on the marketing and strategies, then try to shoehorn the experience around those two things. We have a wealth of systems in the background which are vital for business survival, but often they don't work together to create a seamless experience.

I get it. We're all trying to do what we can with what we've got, and I hate to be the bearer of bad news you don't want to hear— but that approach isn't good enough. The person losing out here is the consumer. When the consumer loses, you lose. Businesses that succeed with experiences first decide what kind of experience they want to provide. Then they make it happen.

No matter how hard we try, we can't reverse engineer happiness. When we take happiness and try to replicate what others did to achieve it, we fail. Happy people figure out what happiness means to them and do what makes them happy. They identify the outcome they want, then design their experience to meet it.

The consumer experience is no different. Design for a specific outcome: how does the customer want to feel? Do they want the superstar feel of an E-Type or the invincible feel of a Defender? *Then* find the kit to match.

Do this the wrong way and you end up with a Frankenstein baby of an experience. It might do the job adequately, but it will do it painfully. It won't ever be true happiness, it won't ever be a true experience. Seth Godin once said, 'If you're going to do it for us, do it beautifully'—and boy, is he right.

When you decide to design for an experience, it's right about the very first step you take that you'll run into your first major challenge. The big problem with consumer experience is it's subjective. Take two people who like similar things, put them in front of the same movie, then give them the same popcorn and the same soda, and they'll *still* leave the movie having had two different experiences. Each person notices different details in the movie, and they have differing opinions of the details. They may even have entirely unique judgements as to whether the movie was good or not. And that's because experience is personal.

We all see the world through our own unique lens. Our lens is exceptional and rare. It's tinted by our past, our memories, our present, our worries and concerns, and our hopes and desires for the future. Every person on this planet wears their own lens, each filtering a different shade of life. This is phenomenal and beautiful—it's one of the true marvels of the human condition.

It also makes marketing a right mess. Marketing would be a *Comedy of Errors* if it weren't for the fact our livelihoods depend on it; instead it's all looking a bit *Romeo and Juliet* where everyone dies and no-one is happy. When every experience is deeply personal, and we each have our own pretty tinted glasses on, businesses are left with an absurd enigma to solve.

Fortunately, we do have some advantages. When you're solving for the impossible the first step is to make *something* possible. Easy-peasy. Breaking it down to what we know already, we know consumers want an extremely personalised experience. Great: let's quantify that.

Ernan Roman, one of the DMA Marketing Hall of Fame inductees, reviewed over 15,000 hours of Voice of Customer research his company ERDM Corp conducted for its clients (including IBM, MassMutual, Microsoft, and QVC) and discovered consumers expect high levels of personalisation, everywhere[2]. He distilled this into seven areas where consumers want specific, personalised engagement:

1. Purchase.
2. On-boarding.
3. Responses to decreasing engagements (e.g. fewer purchases or visits).
4. Immediate responses to negative experiences.

---

2 Roman, E. (2010) *Voice-of-the-Customer Marketing: A Revolutionary 5-Step Process to Create Customers Who Care, Spend, and Stay.* McGraw-Hill Education

5. Surprise and delight thank-yous.

6. Cross-sells and up-sells that add value.

7. Repeat sales and renewals.

That's a lot of personalisation, in a lot of different areas. All those areas combined add up to a person's experience of your products and services and, ultimately, your business. Yet our impossible conundrum is looking more likely now because we have three factors at play: experience = personalisation × (engagement points).

We also know consumers look at life through their tinted lenses—those lenses are the filter of perception. Perception can be defined, broadly speaking, as the sensory information around us plus the baggage of past experience and learned behaviour.

We absorb a great deal of information from around us, and to understand it we pull from our memory the things we've learned over time. This alters how we each perceive events and explains why we all perceive things differently.

Our little rudimentary formula now includes more substantial information: experience = [personalisation × (engagement points)] + perception.

While our experience formula is in no way scientific, it does help us understand the different parts of what we need to solve as a business (don't worry—that's about as much maths as we're going to do).

Perception is a problem for marketers, but luckily we can hack that problem. Psychologists have spent many, many years attempting to figure out how the brain works.

Because psychology has always been perceived as a bit of a 'non-science science', psychologists may have over-compensated a little and produced some phenomenal statistically valid and repeatable research. This is awesome for businesses everywhere.

As psychologists try to unlock why we do what we do, they give us the keys to doors that were never open for us before. We're now able to understand why our customers do such weird things, and we get to apply that understanding to our marketing.

As we learn what the problems are, we can create solutions to fix them. Psychology is the key that enables us to do this.

Behaviour: The Solution

Behaviour is the little thread you can pull to unravel that experience problem. Behaviour allows you to quantify and understand how experience is perceived. If we can quantify a problem, we can design processes to solve for it.

From the seven areas where consumers want personalisation (not to mention all the research done over the years, which we'll get stuck into later), we can see there's a nice outline of a customer journey forming. There's a purchase point and then there's fulfilment.

We also know consumers do a lot of research before they buy. That's the role of advertising. So at a high level there are three basic components to the customer journey: beginning, middle and end.

Right at the beginning is **attention**. Because if the consumer isn't paying attention to their problem, or your adverts, or any of your messages, you can't possibly sell them anything. Everything you want to achieve with your business is impossible without attention. That's your first hurdle—getting and keeping attention.

In the middle, consumers do their research and **decide** what they want to buy. As we'll uncover, that decision process is getting longer and longer.

And at the end you have **purchase** and fulfilment.

So now our three salient points look like this:

- Beginning → Attention.
- Middle → Decision.
- End → Purchase and fulfilment.

Now the consumer journey is forming, and we can see what they want us to personalise within that journey, we can start to create a plan. Add a bit of psychology and you can begin to design for experience. Here's where it gets really interesting, though, because in each of those areas I've listed we hack our own brains.

As I mentioned before, we evolved as a species to survive. We did not evolve to buy things. We evolved to make quick choices. We did not evolve to figure out whether the Defender is better than the E-Type. We simply evolved to live long enough to pass on our genes, then die. This is the brutal truth to life. Everything our brains have evolved to do enables us to simply survive and replicate in the best way possible. Of course, we got cleverer and cleverer over the years, and we began to do things especially well—which ensured we survived even better. Fast forward to today and we're living in an era of unprecedented survival.

However, the modern life we've constructed around us to aide survival means we're using our brains for things they simply weren't designed to do. Ironically, to survive in our current world, we have to hack our survival brains. Because of this, we do some pretty odd things. These odd things impact how we perceive the world around us, and through that our experience. So to craft the experience, businesses need to hack the hacking. Let's look at how the brain is hacking itself.

In The Beginning: Minion Mode

In the beginning there was **attention**. If we don't pay attention to something, it doesn't exist. At least not to us in that moment. The definition of attention in psychology is the concentration of awareness on some phenomenon to the exclusion of other stimuli. Basically, it's the little spotlight of concentration we use to focus on things.

But that's only half the story. Even when we're super-focused on one thing we're still partly paying attention to other things around us—this is peripheral attention. We can never really block everything else out, because that's a silly survival tactic and our brains want us to survive. If we're paying very close attention to something and we hear a lion roar, we'll divert our attention quickly to the sound of the threat, which may well save our lives.

In modern life we use this skill all day, every day so we're able to work *and* keep an eye out for dangers lurking around. The 'cocktail party effect' is the perfect example of this[3]. We can have a conversation with a person in a noisy coffee shop (or a cocktail party for that matter), but if we hear our name across the room our ears suddenly prick up. Understanding how and why this happens is hugely important for understanding how we pay attention, because attention affects everything we do.

This weird duality of attention was first described by Daniel

---

3 Cherry, C. (1953) 'Some experiments on the recognition of speech, with one and with two ears', *Journal of the Acoustical Society of America 25(5)*

Kahneman, who published the much-celebrated book *Thinking Fast and Slow*[4] in 2011. While this is what most people remember him for, the research in the book happened decades before, often with his colleague Amos Tvesrky. Between the two of them, these researchers amassed a wealth of knowledge and understanding about how we pay attention and how that process affects what we do and how we behave.

Kahneman's work has been so influential he was awarded the Nobel prize in Economic Sciences (despite being a psychologist). Kahneman described how we have two systems of thinking, called System 1 and System 2 (inspired!). He was awarded a Nobel prize for the theory because of what this duality of attention does to us when we need to make decisions.

System 1 and System 2 are best exemplified by how we learn to drive. When you first start learning to drive, especially if you have to use gears, it's a thoroughly overwhelming process. There's so much going on at once. You need to control your feet and co-ordinate using your feet with using your hands—without looking at them, because looking at them means you're not looking at the road. Just the process of making the car move in the right direction, at the right speed, and in the right gear is pretty complicated.

Once you've mastered that, however, you also need to pay attention to road signs and the rules of the road. And then you need to pay attention to every other user on the road—most of whom I have come to realise obviously aren't paying attention at all. The first few times you drive are a bewildering, mind-boggling experience. You feel like you're never going to get the hang of it, and you're amazed everyone else does it with such ease.

Skip ahead a few years and driving is a breeze. You hop in the car without hesitation and trundle off down the road like it's no big deal. Sometimes you'll arrive somewhere and have no recollection of getting there at all. Other times you'll accidentally drive to the wrong place and not realise until you get there. How terrifying, when you remember you're driving at least a tonne's worth of death machine!

In these scenarios you might say to yourself, 'Damn, I wasn't paying attention'—but that's where you're wrong. We're always paying

---

4 Kahneman, D. (2011) *Thinking, Fast and Slow*, Penguin

attention—the only time we're not is when we're asleep. You weren't paying the right kind of attention, though, and that's what matters.

When you first learn to drive, operating a car requires all your attention. Very focused attention. That kind of focused attention is System 2. It's the more deliberate part of our minds. Kahneman likens it to a pilot: the pilot allows us to focus and give effortful attention to something. System 2 is controlled and highly cognitive, and we mostly use it to solve problems. This system is what really saved our skins when we were scrabbling around in the dirt because it allowed us to invent weapons and fire.

System 1, on the other hand, is responsible for getting you to where you want to go safely, once you've learned to drive. When you're lost in thought and suddenly arrive at your destination, it's System 1 that got you there. System 1 is your autopilot. It takes a long time to learn to do something complicated, but once you've learned it and it's a habit, System 1 takes over.

System 1 is always on. Always. And because System 1 constantly runs in the background, when your name is mentioned, your ears will prick up—despite the fact you're having an engaging conversation you're paying full attention to. System 1 hears your name and instructs you to divert some of your attention away because something important is happening over there.

System 1 is often referred to as being automatic. It's running all the time looking out for things, and when it sees what it's looking for it reacts super-fast. System 1 keeps us alive. It has evolved to be quick and make intuitive decisions without thinking.

That automatic functionality is so crucial because the system needs to be efficient. When we face danger, we can't afford to 'uhm' and 'ah' about the best course of action—if we do, the lion will eat us before we've decided what to do. We need to act now. That's System 1's job: to save time and effort.

System 2, on the other hand, is very deliberate. It works through things step by step. This makes System 2 flexible and gives it the ability to solve problems and make considered decisions to great effect—but it also makes the brain slow. Being slow is a problem for survival.

That's not the only problem though: System 2 is hugely cognitively demanding. It uses lots of resources, and the brain doesn't like that. A large drain on resources means there's less to go around the rest of the body, which is another problem for survival. The brain does not like using System 2, so if it can use System 1 instead, it will.

Phil Barden put this beautifully: 'In a way, the brain is not made for thinking, but for fast and automatic actions.'[5]

The real difference between the two systems is in how much information they can absorb. System 2—the pilot, our complex problem solver—takes in around forty bits of information per second. System 1, on the other hand—our autopilot—takes in around eleven million bits of information per second. The discrepancy is huge.

We like to think we spend all our time in System 2, fully in control, a pilot of our own destiny—but the reality is, the brain is lazy. It's trying to save resources and keep us alive. And so System 1 is where it's at: we're on autopilot most of the time.

Estimates vary as to how much of the day we spend in System 1, but it's generally accepted from various neuro-marketing studies that we coast along on autopilot between eighty per cent and ninety per cent of the day[6].

The autopilot can only take in so much information and govern so much of our lives without consciously paying attention to any of it by doing a little bit of hacking itself. The autopilot makes associative judgements to make decisions. In other words, if our autopilot brain has done that exact thing before—and it knows what to do—it just does it. If System 1 has done something *similar* before and it can use the same behaviour, then it will use that action, whatever that action is. In other words, System 1 uses rules of thumb to decide what to do.

If we've not encountered a particular scenario before, like learning to drive a car, dealing with the new situation gets bumped up to the pilot (System 2). But once you have some rules in place for what you need to do, the autopilot says, 'I can handle that' and frees up the pilot to think about something else. When driving becomes habitual, the autopilot takes over entirely. The brain preserves energy and becomes

5 Barden, P. (2013) *Decoded: The Science Behind Why We Buy*. John Wiley & Sons
6 Mahoney, M. (2003) *The Subconscious Mind of the Consumer (And How To Reach It)* Harvard Business School Working Knowledge

extremely efficient, and these rules of thumb mean the autopilot can handle huge amounts of data, every second of your waking day.

The problem with System 1—the autopilot—is it makes mistakes. Sometimes it creates associations between the wrong things and decides on the wrong action. Which is what happens when you hop in the car, get preoccupied, and drive to your office instead of to the critical meeting you're supposed to attend. Or if you put the ice cream by the couch and the remote control in the fridge when you're tired.

The big problem for businesses is the mistakes System 1 makes often have negative consequences for you. For instance, when a consumer visits your website, the autopilot forms an impression of the site with every bit of sensory information it receives—the design, colour scheme, and content—within a second. It may take much longer to actively consume the site's content, but the impression is already there, and that impression will hugely influence the consumer's behaviour. This associative power is intuitive, it's what gives us the 'gut' feel people often talk about.

We have no conscious access to the autopilot, so it communicates and influences us without us realising.

Looking at the average interaction times with advertising we can see most of the processing doesn't even have time to pass up to our conscious brain, the pilot[7].

The autopilot decides what to do with it first:

- Advert in a magazine: 1.7 seconds.
- Poster: 1.5 seconds.
- Mail: 2 seconds.
- Banner ad: 1 second.

Marketing must either deliver its message within seconds or be so disruptive the pilot has to take over. You run the risk of being filtered out completely by the autopilot if you don't match its relevancy criteria for one of its rules of thumb. As a business, you talk to your prospects' autopilot most of the time. You target the efficient hack the brain uses to filter the world.

Since releasing his dual system theory, Kahneman's data has been

---

7 Barden, P. (2013) *Decoded: The Science Behind Why We Buy*, John Wiley & Sons

replicated hundreds of times, supported by neuroscience. This has led to vast quantities of research in the field.

What we now know is these rules of thumb (also called heuristics) can be split into different categories. Those categories then lead to specific short-cuts the brain uses. These short-cuts are called cognitive biases. There are three rules of thumb that are of particular importance to marketing:

- The Representativeness Heuristic.
- The Availability Heuristic.
- The Anchoring Heuristic.

The Representativeness Heuristic

This rule of thumb is all about categorical segmentation in which we create prototypes for categories. A prototype is an example that matches the category best.

For instance, if we think of old people, we might think of a grandfather and grandmother. A specific person comes to mind. We understand what 'old people' are by bringing specific individuals—the grandfather and grandmother—to the forefront of our attention. Doing this helps us understand the world more easily and with less effort.

We have categories for everything, and for each category we have a prototype. Each time we encounter something that fits a certain category we compare it to the prototype, which is our brain's representation of the category. To understand something we need to make a comparison, which forms our frame of reference. However, this method is prone to error. If we see old people, and our prototype is of a kindly old grandparent couple, we automatically assume all the old people we see are also kindly—which is why it's easier for juries to send a young man to prison for war crimes than it is to send an 85-year-old Nazi to prison for the same crimes. Prototyping also gives rise to stereotypes. If you run into computer problems and you go to the IT department, you're likely to head for the youngest male in the room. That's the stereotype assigned to techies.

This heuristic can unfortunately spread gender stereotyping and discrimination, making it difficult for certain people and groups to break into careers, so it sometimes needs pushing back.

The Availability Heuristic

This is the tendency to judge how likely something is to happen by whether or not you can bring it to mind easily.

If your consumer needs to make a decision and can readily bring examples to the front of their mind, they'll perceive that it's more likely they can achieve what they want to do—which means you're far more likely to get a 'yes'.

If your customer doesn't have these examples they may believe they can't do it, or they'll believe it's too hard and decide not to do it. This is why case studies are more important than most business owners realise. It's also why repeating themes works so well in content creation, because repetition helps your audience become more familiar with what you're doing.

The availability heuristic becomes a problem when it gives rise to biases such as the false consensus effect—which is when we think our own opinions are the most common in the general population[8]. A study by Ross, Green, and House (1977) showed whatever choices the participants in their study made, they assumed the majority of other people would do the same[9].

The consensus effect is a particular problem around election time because if we all think our opinion is the most commonly held opinion, we close ourselves to what other people may think and feel. This can lead to racial prejudice, homophobia, and other nasties being considered "normal"—which is exactly what's happened during recent political upheavals in the UK and the United States.

This false consensus bias happens because self-belief is easy to recall from memory because self-belief belongs to us. Because it's our own information, it's the easiest information to remember. We recall our own opinions and emotions before we look to remember information from other sources.

We put undue weighting on this personal information merely

8 Gross, S.R. & Miller, N. (1997) 'The "Golden Section" and bias in perceptions of social consensus', *Personality and Social Psychology Review*, 1(3), 241–71
9 Ross, L., Green, D., & House, P. (1977) The 'false consensus effect': An egocentric bias in social perception and attribution processes. *Journal of Experimental Social Psychology*, 13, 279–301.

because it's available, without critically evaluating it. Because of this, we think everyone is more likely to agree with our opinions.

The Anchoring Heuristic

This is similar to the availability heuristic because it's based on the same principle of available information; the twist is we're biased towards the starting value when we make quantitative judgements.

The first piece of information we take in acts as an anchor and sets the baseline for the next piece of information. The first piece is the most readily available information for what's currently happening.

Greenberg et al (1986) put together a mock jury to test this theory[10]. They found that participants who were first asked to think about a heavy sentence for someone on trial handed down a much harsher punishment than another group, who were asked to think about a lighter sentence first. The second group of participants sentenced much more leniently because their anchor—their frame of reference— was a much more lenient punishment.

This demonstrates why it's good to use a higher price as an anchor when displaying pricing options. Your customers will see the high price first—then when they come to the option they want, your price will seem much lower in comparison. You have the power to set your own baseline.

There are hundreds more biases out there, with more being discovered all the time. Biases can, however, be grouped together depending on the action the brain wants to take:

- What we should remember.
- The need to act fast.
- Too much information.
- Not enough meaning.

Let's sum up what happens at the beginning, when you're trying to get your consumers' attention.

First you need to get past the gatekeeper—the autopilot. Get past

---

10 Greenberg, J., Williams, K.D., & O'Brien, M.K. 'Considering the harshest verdict first: biasing effects on mock juror verdicts.' *Personality and Social Psychology Bulletin* vol 12(1) 41–50

that and you'll have won the first battle: your customer's attention. Then you must retain that attention so you can help your customer make a decision. Remember: you have little time, and you'll be compared to a prototype for the category you're operating in. You can take control by differentiating yourself enough to stand out from everyone else in your category.

Secondly, the availability heuristic will come into play if you're trying to get someone to take action. Show your customer proof that what you do works, and you'll be able to overcome that challenge.

Third, anchoring means a baseline will be set for comparison: so own that baseline. Once you're in control as much as possible, educate the consumer's autopilot. Build positive associations with your business so you become a trusted source for consumers and they don't filter you out.

I like to think of the pilot and the autopilot in terms of the minions from *Despicable Me* (if you've not watched this movie, it's very silly and enjoyable and you should watch it immediately). The pilot is like Gru— he's the overlord. He simply can't do all the things he needs to do, so he employs a race of helpers: the minions. These little guys, who are bright yellow but not very bright, are the autopilot. There are hundreds of them, and they each have a specific job. One simple job per minion.

Mostly the minions trundle along just fine, but every now and then something goes wrong and chaos ensues. Generally it's because they've been given something to handle that doesn't fit their "one minion, one job" criteria. Your advertising, content, and website need to be minion-friendly. If you're not minion-friendly you will get filtered out, because your consumers spend a good eighty to ninety per cent of the day in minion mode.

In The Middle: Hard Choices

Once you're past the gatekeeper you've cleared the first hurdle. At this point you're still in the running and you haven't been filtered out. That means you're minion-friendly and you've done a great job! This is no time to rest on your laurels though, because here's where you start to get judged for that elusive experience.

The problem is we all believe we're logical beings capable of weighing up all the information at hand and making the best choice possible. Unfortunately, as we've just discovered, because we're coasting along in autopilot mode being run by minions, we can throw 'logical' out the window.

Freedom of choice may very well be an illusion. The rules of thumb we use mean there really is no such thing as free choice. When given options to choose from we hardly make the most appropriate ones, because we choose based on logical errors. We make mistakes.

Ultimately, because of our autopilot, we need help to make good decisions. You can provide an awesome experience for people coming into your business by making it easy for them to make their decision. The autopilot likes everything to be tangible, immediate, and certain:

- Tangibility: there must be tangible and obvious signals for your autopilot to get the hint that it needs to take an action.
- Immediacy: the autopilot prefers immediate rewards rather than future ones.
- Certainty: the autopilot prefers the safe, certain choice over the risky, uncertain one.

In their fabulous book on choice architecture, *Nudge*, Thaler and Sunstein talk about helping people make decisions[11]. They propose that when a decision is made you should structure the decision nicely so it's easier for the consumer to act upon. Here's a summary of when you know you need to help:

- *When there is some kind of incentive involved.* That means the autopilot goes after pleasure now and worries about the cost later, which can lead to serious regrets down the line.
- *Whenever there is a hard choice.* The autopilot rejects the hard choice in favour of an easier choice. If it chooses based on that criterion, it often makes the wrong choice.
- *If the option doesn't happen frequently.* The autopilot won't know what to do with your option if it's never seen it before, and will freeze up or ignore the choice.
- *When someone has little understanding of the effects of their*

---

11 Thaler, R.H., & Sunstein, C.R. (2009) *Nudge: Improving Decisions About Health, Wealth and Happiness*. Penguin

choice. If your consumer is confused or overwhelmed, they won't make a choice at all. Break things down and make it easy to choose.

If your product or service falls into any of those four areas, you'll need to help your customer decide what to do. Helping them boils down to making the choice easy, clear, and simple.

If the purchase is in one of those four areas, consumers will do research to help them make a decision before they buy or commit. If you show up just when they're doing that research and looking for help, you have the opportunity to get past the autopilot and help them decide—which is what a good experience does.

This is the role decent content fulfils in marketing. Making a decision is a cumulative process, where the consumer builds knowledge and collects information. But the consumer doesn't know what you know, and won't necessarily make the right choices. You can help them with that. You can provide:

- Tangibility with good quality, value-added content.
- Immediacy with positive progression through their buying decision.
- Certainty by building trust and a relationship.

This is where you design and craft the experience. There is an entire journey for this, which we'll get to soon.

At The End: Rewards

Once you've helped your customer with the decision process, make sure the act of purchasing is a lovely experience, too. Intriguingly, the act of buying is probably where we hack our brains the most. This has serious ramifications for product positioning, pricing, and marketing, which all affect the buyer experience.

In 2007, neuroscientist Brian Knutson used an fMRI scanner to observe brain activity when making purchase decisions[12]. He wanted to see if he could predict purchase behaviour by looking at what the brain was doing.

---

12 Knutson, B., Rick, S., Wimmer, G.E., Prelec, D., & Loewenstein, G. (2007) 'Neural Predictors of Purchases', *Neuron*, Vol 53(1), pp 147–56

Knutson asked people to look at some images—the first showed the product, the second showed the price—after which consumers state whether or not they would buy the product. When participants saw the product, the brain's reward centres lit up. This makes sense because we know this area of the brain is triggered when we value something. So if we value a product the brain's reward centre fires up. The more we value a product, the higher the activation; conversely, the less we value it, the lower the activation.

What was really interesting was what happened when the participants saw the price. An entirely different, and unexpected, area of the brain lit up: the insula. This area of the brain normally activates when we feel physical or emotional pain. Buying things—parting with money—hurts. We didn't evolve to buy things, so to understand pricing we have to hack the brain.

Giving away resources (in this case paying for something with money) is a cost the brain is reluctant to incur because parting with resources is not good for survival. So when we see a price, the brain registers it in a similar way as we would pain. Understanding good value is easier for us, because the brain rewards us when we do things to aid our survival. It punishes us by emulating pain when we do things that put our survival at risk—like paying for things.

Equally interesting was Knutson's discovery that he could predict whether or not someone would purchase an item *before* they said yes or no. If the amount of reward activation outweighed the pain activation, a person was highly likely to buy. If the pain was greater than the reward, they wouldn't. This gave Knutson a handy little formula:

Net Value = Reward − Pain

The key here is to increase the reward you offer. You can reduce the pain somewhat, but it will always be there; you can't eliminate the pain of paying altogether. Any time a consumer has to pay for something, they'll experience pain because that's simply how we understand cost. Aim to make the net value of your product or service as high as is feasible. The pleasure of the value must outweigh the pain of paying for it, or the purchase is unlikely to happen at all.

Businesses whose customers happily buy from them understand how to play the reward–pain game. When we're designing the buying experience, we can use strategies to help us with this. You'll find out more about these as you read this book.

The Hacking

Whether a consumer is deciding to buy or actually buying, once you're past the autopilot and have their attention, you need to add value. 'Add value' is your new mantra. You can hack the hacking by understanding precisely how to add value and create a journey that takes each salient point of the purchase into consideration. That journey is your crafted experience.

By taking the best ideas from buyer psychology you can make sure you hack the hacking the brain is already doing. In order to do that effectively and touch all the salient points you need a framework. But not just any old framework; you need one that includes your hacking points.

In the next chapters, we'll discuss this framework and how it ties in with this section. But first, let's take a look at real-life applications of what we've been discussing here—a framework that takes behaviour into consideration.

Behaviour: Real Life

Because we're all human, creating behavioural journeys works for both B2B and B2C companies. Below you'll find two examples of this from our own clients. The first is a B2B company and the second a B2C powerhouse.

James Birch runs Colour Graphics with his dad. Colour Graphics is a phenomenal printing business producing some amazing high-quality products on amazing high-quality machines. We were originally introduced because James needed a little help getting his Infusionsoft by Keap application working with Magento, an eCommerce solution. While we were chatting I realised James had a far bigger problem than just connecting the two pieces of software: he had no customer journey planned whatsoever. The more I dug, the more we uncovered.

It wasn't that James was running a shoddy show. Not at all. Colour Graphics was comfortable, and it was profitable. They hit an annual turnover of £1.2m—which was great. However, James wanted to get to

£2m but growth had plateaued. James had a solid customer base, most of whom repeated their purchases at relatively frequent intervals. This was proof of the company's quality and customer service because they didn't have any loyalty campaigns running to bring consumers back for more. Digging a little deeper we found there wasn't much clarity on who their ideal customer was. That was a problem, as it meant we couldn't understand any of the behaviour well enough to create a behavioural journey.

The third issue was an astronomical bounce rate from the website.

After troubleshooting the various problem areas and looking at the goals we wanted to achieve, we created a plan. First, be clear on who we're dealing with so we can target and nurture appropriately. Second, capture and convert more leads. And third, nurture more reliable customer loyalty.

Taking these points into consideration, the first focus was getting clarity on the target audience. James worked his way through our avatar course, and by the end we had a clear idea of his ideal customer. Then we crafted a plan for each point of the customer journey. This took his consumers from the initial attention phase through to loyalty and advocacy. With the journey planned out we realigned focus: first, getting more leads and converting them, and second, building rapport and relationships with existing consumers to get loyalty.

The website bounces were a problem. The traffic was fine, but visitors were leaving without taking action. On reviewing the competition, the bounce rate was more than likely caused by a price pain. Colour Graphics isn't cheap, but the high quality of the printing comes at a higher price. So we needed to educate consumers and show them why the price was justified.

Our strategy was to put an exit intent pop-up on the site, offering a coupon code delivered via email and followed by an email series welcoming the new lead, showing them why Colour Graphics was more expensive than some other suppliers.

That campaign alone outperformed even our wildest hopes. I thought conservatively it would convert at around 10 per cent; 15 per cent if we were lucky because of the coupon code. The new lead campaign consistently converts at between 48 per cent and 52 per cent.

It's phenomenal. And the campaign is evergreen, so every month new people come in, netting James an additional £30,000 or so monthly.

At the other end of the process is loyalty. From the new lead campaign consumers move to the new customer campaign. There, they convert to a second sale at around 12 per cent. After that we keep them warm, and when they hit a certain threshold the loyalty campaign kicks off.

The loyalty campaign is simple—it's a personal email from James thanking them for being a loyal customer. They then get a coupon code for their next order, should they choose to use it. It's not pushy, it's not fancy, it's a super personal thank you. The campaign converts at around 40 per cent and brings in approximately an additional £10,000 a month.

The beauty of these campaigns is their simplicity. You don't have to go overboard with your customer journey to make it work. The messages themselves don't have to be complicated; the complexity is in the appropriate timing and orchestrating when you send them. A lot happens behind the scenes to track the customer's journey and make sure they are spoken to appropriately and catered for at each point, but the approach is simple: cater to the experience—Colour Graphics cares. These simple campaigns smashed James's goal of £2m turnover. That's the power of a behavioural experience for a B2B company.

On the consumer side of this journey is the lovely Mike Browne. As well as being a phenomenal human being, Mike owns Picture This (Imaging) Ltd. On the surface it's a business selling photography courses, workshops and training.

But Mike's company is so much more than that. Watch just a few of Mike's YouTube videos (his channel has 250,000 subscribers) and you realise what he does best is ignite and stoke a passion in hobbyist photographers. He shows people how to take pictures, but the journey he takes them on is about so much more than just photographs and cameras.

When Mike and I first met he wanted to automate his business. He needed it streamlined and converting better. With all the courses he'd created, and the amazing videos he's produced over the years, Mike's dream was to put them all together in such a way that students could progress through the various skill levels in a similar way to working through a curriculum. It very quickly became apparent he didn't only need automation. Yes, he wanted an automated journey, but he also needed to put in place a behavioural journey.

So along with my team, Mike and I put our heads together and designed a behavioural journey worthy of the care and consistency of quality that Mike provides his students. The curriculum cascade was crafted, and we set up the courses to be delivered via a drip-fed online membership platform. There was a lot to automate, but we were working towards the end goal of having a behavioural system in place.

It took time. There was a lot to move and consolidate, and there was reams of content to create. We had to build an entire membership site. But once these systems were in place, we finally started installing some content into the process. We took the videos Mike had on YouTube and designed a long-term nurture process to trickle content out over a period of weeks. To simulate how Mike interacts with his customers in person, we ensured there was a backbone of content in place. The plan was to make sure no consumer could ever be left behind; everyone got looked after.

That nurture-forward approach doubled Mike's open rates. By always looking to increase the value-add and the perceived experience, Mike was welcomed into inboxes the world over. Because we didn't focus on one campaign in isolation, the experience for the consumer is accumulative. The nurture-forward approach to Mike's marketing has doubled his course sales over the last two years.

Now we've achieved that will we stop? Absolutely not. We can always improve the experience, and currently we're working on automated engagement triggers and personalisation. It's continual optimisation, a never-ending process of refining and tweaking to ensure Mike grows with his consumers and vice versa. The relationship Mike has with his customers and his care for their journey should be the standard every business aims for.

Behaviour: The Science & The Data

As we progress through this book, we'll cover what you can do to add value to the consumer journey so you know exactly how to design and provide an amazing experience. For now, I'd like to share with you

GREEN YELLOW RED BLACK
BLACK RED GREEN ORANGE
PURPLE YELLOW BLUE BLUE
RED YELLOW ORANGE BLUE
YELLOW BLUE BLACK RED
BLUE YELLOW BLACK ORANGE
GREEN PURPLE RED YELLOW
BLUE GREEN YELLOW BLUE
BLACK BLACK PURPLE RED
ORANGE YELLOW BLUE GREEN
PURPLE BLACK RED YELLOW
BLACK RED YELLOW GREEN
YELLOW PURPLE BLACK ORANGE

Fig 1: Stroop test (conflict)

how the brain decides between using System 1 or System 2, and what happens when it can't decide.

What happens when System 1 and System 2 fight? Mostly the systems trundle along and work together nicely. But every so often they'll reach a point of conflict. Take a look at Figure 1 over the page. The idea is to move through the columns, as quickly as possible, saying only the colour of the word out loud (rather than the word itself). Have a little try; I'll wait.

While the premise is simple, in practice it's actually quite demanding. That's because you've just made the pilot and the autopilot have an argument. The autopilot can easily understand the word. It has no problem with that, and it can do the same with colours.

But put the two together and make the meaning of the word and the colour of the text conflict and the autopilot gets upset. At that point the pilot needs to step in and take over. Each word cycle repeats again, the autopilot in conflict and the pilot overriding.

This takes a lot of cognitive effort. Most tests get easier the longer you go on, because you figure out the method and the autopilot takes over. With this test, that can't happen, so the struggle continues. The longer you go on, the more you need to concentrate in order to not make a mistake. The pilot starts exhausting the brain and using all the resources, and so the autopilot tries to kick in and you make even more mistakes. This devious little gem is the Stroop test and it's ingeniously designed.

However, it wasn't designed to show off Systems 1 and 2, it was designed a full forty years ago by John Ridley Stroop. It's the most famous test in the history of psychology, and it just so happens it perfectly displays the roles of the two systems. This conflict is what happens when the way you look and sound as a business is vastly different from how you operate. Don't do this to your consumers.

If System 1 and 2 get into conflict, how does the brain choose which one to use? If you understand how the brain chooses, you can identify when your consumers will struggle in each of the systems, which means you can prepare the right strategy to deploy. Interestingly, the choice is not just about resource use. In 1996, Kruglanski put together a model called the motivated tactician[13]. He argued we strategically allocate resources depending on four variables:

- Time.
- Cognitive load.
- Importance.
- Information.

First, if we don't have time, we'll default to the autopilot. If we do have time, we'll use some of our precious pilot resources.

Second, if we're busy and have a lot on our minds, the autopilot will handle the task without us having to divert resources.

13 Kruglanski, A.W. (1996) Motivated social cognition: principles of the interface. In E. T. Higgins & A. W. Kruglanski (Eds.) *Social psychology: Handbook of basic principles* pp 493-520. Guilford

Third, if the decision is super-important and requires lots of logical, detailed answers, the pilot has to do it. The autopilot is only happy to provide estimates.

And, finally, if we have all the information we need, the autopilot can make things happen. But if the information isn't there, we'll either do nothing or find more information and again the pilot has to get involved.

What's so important here is even if the conditions are right for the pilot to take work on, the brain doesn't want to do that. So it might just filter the information out and do nothing at all. This risks important information being lost to the trash—your business included.

To stop this from happening you can control each of these four areas as much as possible, which means controlling the desired outcome as much as possible. This is your first step to crafting an experience—quantifying behaviour.

With that in mind, Chapter 2 looks at the framework we need to use to create an admirable behavioural journey.

The Brain Hack

The brain uses rules and mental shortcuts to make sense of the world. To do this, it runs two systems: System 1 and System 2.

System 1 is the autopilot, and it's always on. It uses associations and rules of thumb to understand the world and filters out any information it considers irrelevant. It is easily confused, and often makes mistakes.

System 2 is slow, it works on hard problems, and it uses a lot of energy. The brain uses System 2 only when it has no other option and dislikes doing so because it uses precious resources.

The interplay of these two systems leads to odd quirks and biases.

Hack Your Buyer's Brain

If you want to hack your buyer's brain, provide an experience the autopilot understands and finds easy. Consider the 7 areas customers want personalisation.

Don't overload the brain, help it be lazy. Throughout this experience provide:

- Tangibility
- Immediacy
- Certainty

Work on satisfying the components of the purchase formula:

$$Net\ value = Reward - Pain$$

CHAPTER 2: Lifecycle Marketing

"Aim for the sky, but move slowly, enjoying every step along the way. It is all those little steps that make the journey complete."

~ Chanda Kochhar

CHAPTER 2: Lifecycle Marketing

Lifecycle Marketing: The Principle & The Problem

I've already written about how experience is everything, and how it will be the main differentiator for the future—more than price or quality. But let's look at what experience is doing for businesses now. Companies that prioritise customer experience generate 60 per cent higher profits than their competitors[1]. This is all kinds of good. So let's look at how you nail the ghost-like nature of experience to the wall.

It's all in the planning.

The customer experience doesn't just need to be good, it needs to be repeatable. Dependable. You need to know you can achieve the outcomes you want every time. And you can only do that if you have a plan that takes repeatability and dependability into consideration. Businesses that succeed plan for targeted customer behaviour from the start. Plan for your customers' happiness and do it across the entire lifetime of the relationship with your consumer.

---

1 Reference: Murphy, E.C., & Murphy, M.A. (2002) *Leading on the Edge of Chaos: The 10 Critical Elements for Success in Volatile Times*. Prentice Hall Press

Your plan must account for the journey your consumer will take. That journey needs to be engaging, it needs to add value, and it needs to build a connection. Your end goal is to build a relationship with prospective customers through a carefully crafted experience. Customer loyalty and raving fans are built through strong ties to a company that's genuinely improved their lives. The effect an experience has on the most loyal customers is remarkable—which is what we need to aim for.

In summary: you need to craft a repeatable plan that, by targeting specific yet personal customer behaviour, creates a positive effect on your customer's life through their experience of coming into contact with you. Bloody hell, right? And those key words have popped up again: repeatable, consistent, and remarkable experience.

This, of course, seems totally overwhelming and unobtainable at first. Finding the starting point on your own journey to creating good customer experiences seems messy and complicated which is compounded by the reams of conflicting information out there. We're all busy enough as it is, without having to fight with conflicting advice and craft a customer journey based on perception and opinion. It actually feels like we're setting ourselves up for failure.

As of the time of writing this book, more than 70 million new blog posts are created each month. There are 1.7 billion websites on our lovely internet[2]. That's three or four per internet user. That is a heck of a lot of information. How we consume that information has changed. We're no longer content to use only one device at a time. Using multiple devices, such as a smartphone and a laptop together, has become the norm. This is called second-screening. We're fracturing our attention.

I saw a beautiful example of this on a train in the UK. Sitting at the table across from me was a very busy lady. She had the following arranged in front of her:

- Two smartphones.
- A laptop.
- A notebook.
- A tablet.

---

2 WordPress (2018) https://wordpress.com/activity/

I watched her for a while.

She had one of the smartphones propped up and was watching something on it. She had her headphones in and seemed to be listening. She had her laptop open to some spreadsheets she was working on. Her tablet displayed a document she was referencing. Every now and then, she'd jot down a quick note on the notebook. Her second phone would buzz, and she'd type a quick message before turning back to the spreadsheet on the laptop and the document on the tablet.

Five items all occupying her attention. Seemingly effortlessly.

Another common second-screening habit is a bit closer to home. In the evening, I like to watch TV as my first wind down, followed by a book in bed. If the programme is moving slowly, or adverts come on, I often find myself on my phone researching something, chatting, or even watching another video. The busy lady on the train and I are not alone. As Tim Elkington, of the Internet Advertising Bureau, observes:

"Second-screening is ingrained to such a degree that all screens are now equal. There's no hierarchy, only fragmentation of attention— actually, switch-screening is a much more accurate term."

Here's where two major influences collide: the availability of information and how we consume it. We have more information at our finger tips, and more ways than ever to absorb it. So, yes: there's been a massive shift. A big change. But it's not the end of the world. It just means we no longer have as much control as we thought we had.

I say *thought*, because when we look back at the paragraphs on opinion and the perception of experience, it's not clear that we ever did have much control. Very simply, the buyer controls the relationship. And it's now evident that is the case. We might be overwhelmed with how to stay on top of all of it, but consumers are not—they're demanding we as business owners do better.

"I use a search engine very often to guide, advise, or inform a personal decision (big or small). I use search this way to find the most accurate information quickly. When I search, I expect results to be personalised and/or relevant to me." (Deborah H., 51)

What intrigues me most about this quote is Deborah's age. Deborah was 51 when she said it. Most people assume—incorrectly—that those consumers who turn to the internet for everything are mostly millennials. Deborah is not a millennial.

This behaviour is found across all age groups. Consumers want instant access to the information they need, and they want the information personalised. This means your consumers want access to the information in your head, and they want access to your knowledge. You have a huge opportunity to help your consumers make good decisions. It's your chance to start the journey with them on the right foot, by adding value.

At this point, most business owners run off and start creating reams of content: blog posts, podcasts, videos, articles... But they're missing the point entirely. While creating content is great—and you should be doing it—consumers don't want just *any* content. They want personalised content, information that's relevant and unique to them in their moment of need, specific to the problem they currently face.

Lifecycle Marketing: The Solution

There are three major, immediate problems:

- You need a good, strong customer experience for an ever-more discerning and demanding consumer base.
- You're fighting for your customer's fractured attention.
- You need to grab attention and create the customer experience in a dependable way.

What's a business to do?

First, you need a plan. Craft an experience and systematise it. Then take back some control and create experiences that allow you to target specific customer behaviours and keep customer attention. Be there when your customers need you most with relevant, personalised information that helps them, then continue the relationship by planning for future behaviour. Add value and cultivate a positive connection with quality information for each of the little steps towards the consumer's end goal.

This is how you become proactive instead of reactive for those customers who expect personalisation and a remarkable experience.

But how do you do that exactly? Well, here's the good news: despite the fact we're all such special snowflakes, every human goes through specific stages when buying something. This is the same whether you're business-to-business, business-to-consumer, business-to-government, or a charity. It's the same whatever you're selling. And it's the same across cultures and continents.

We call these buying stages the awareness journey, and every stage in the journey must be satisfied for a purchase to occur. The stronger a customer's relationship with you, the shorter the stages. The smaller the purchase, the shorter the stages.

The bigger the purchase, the longer the stages. The more decision-makers involved, the more complex the interplay between stages.

If you want to craft a meaningful experience for your customer, understand their behaviour. Nailing their awareness journey is vital. Here are the stages:

- ↓ Unaware
- ↓ Awareness
- ↓ Consideration
- ↓ Decision
- ↓ Retain (Enjoyment)
- ↓ Loyalty
- ↓ Attrition and Re-engagement
- ↓ (Apathy or Unhappy)

To convert your prospects into customers, you must understand this journey and put a structure in place to account for it. So, to touch on each of the awareness points—do we need a system? Aha! Let me introduce you to lifecycle marketing.

Lifecycle marketing is a framework designed to make it easy to implement these stages into a system. It's platform—and business-category agnostic, too, so anyone can apply it in their business. Lifecycle marketing was originally created by the team at Infusionsoft by Keap, specifically to help small businesses systemise their sales and marketing in the customer-journey framework. It's designed to cover top-, middle- and bottom-of-funnel activities.

Top-of-funnel activities are those designed to attract and collect leads. Middle-of-funnel activities are those which engage and nurture your leads. And bottom-of-funnel activities are crafted to convert and satisfy your customers.

Funnily enough, these top-, middle- and bottom-funnel activities look remarkably like the awareness journey I've just described, right?

That's because they are. The top-, middle- and bottom-funnel concept is a simplified version of the awareness journey.

Here's how the two fit together:

TOP OF FUNNEL
- ↓ Unaware
- ↓ Awareness

MIDDLE OF FUNNEL
- ↓ Consideration

BOTTOM OF FUNNEL
- ↓ Decision
- ↓ Retain (Enjoyment)
- ↓ Loyalty
- ↓ Attrition and Re-engagement
- ↓ (Apathy or Unhappy)

The more you dig into the origins of marketing strategies, the more you realise everything in the marketing industry is recycled or reinvented. Nothing is 100 per cent original.

Infusionsoft by Keap took some of these marketing concepts and made them accessible to small businesses, so their target audience could put repeatable systems in place and earn good return on investment (ROI) on their software and services.

I love its simplicity and ease of implementation.

The key differentiator for this framework over other marketing strategies, is lifecycle marketing allows you to intelligently market to your prospects and customers alike. The focus is on helping you create meaningful relationships by understanding the value of the *entirety* of the customer lifecycle, not just their current purchase.

As the name suggests, lifecycle marketing focuses on the entire customer experience, from first contact all the way through to customer acquisition and retention, and on to loyalty. It doesn't drop off after you make the sale—rather, it helps you keep each customer and keep them buying from you.

The aim was to help business owners realise the potential in their customer bases after the point of first purchase, then use simple strategies and tactics in a single, self-sustaining process, to turn one-off customers into repeat buyers and brand advocates. Although aimed at small businesses, any size of company can use the framework—titans included. It's a three-phase framework comprising Attract–Sell–Wow, as shown in Figure 2.

Each of the phases then breaks down to three further sections, which we'll come to later. The significance of the framework is not in its individual phases, or their subsections, but rather the focus—attracting, selling, and wowing your customer base—and how each stage interplays with the others to achieve a well-rounded system.

You don't have to be an Infusionsoft by Keap user, or even have an online business, to use this framework. It's system-, industry-, business-model, and platform-agnostic. And that's because the tactics

Fig 2: Attract-Sell-Wow model

47

it advocates have been used in business in some shape or form for thousands of years. (Nothing is new, eh?)

The key to lifecycle marketing's simplicity is its modular nature, which allows you to create real customer journeys. Lifecycles are not linear and prospects do not behave in a linear manner because we're all human. This is why many older marketing models are outdated and simply fail to perform. As Marketo says:

"Some buyers go through the same stage multiple times, some skip a stage, and some may revert back to an older stage before taking two steps forward. In the past, it was hard for marketers to identify individuals in the journey, let alone react to where they are in the journey. That's changed, however, with the emergence of more sophisticated marketing automation platforms and complementary technologies, and the model needs to evolve to reflect that reality."[3]

Over years of implementing this framework, I found the three phases were simply not enough, so I added another one. Not enough focus and attention was given to the engagement part of the awareness journey—and in today's hyper-connected and attention-fractured world, engagement needs to be the predominant focus.

And, of course, I've added our own behavioural slant to the entire process, which means you can have customer behaviour drive the

Fig 3: Attract-Engage-Sell-Wow model

---

3 *The Business Case for Customer Experience Investment*, Netcall Telecom Limited, https://www.netcall.com/files/2016-03-10/eguidecustomer-experience-investmentnetcallfinal-D0jI.pdf

model. And that is marketing Nirvana.

The phase I added in was **Engage**. The lifecycle marketing model includes three phases: Attract–Sell–Wow. The Automation Ninjas adaptation makes that: Attract–Engage–Sell–Wow, as shown in Figure 3. This is a phase Infusionsoft by Keap has considered adding for some time now, and we couldn't agree more. Marketo thinks engagement is so important it call its entire marketing strategy 'engagement marketing'.

In today's fickle marketplace, your business is nothing without customer and prospect engagement. It's what makes your customers stick around. At a basic level, lifecycle marketing starts with reaching your target market and progresses towards creating an established, loyal customer base. We'll cover each of the stages in the basics here, and later on I'll show you exactly how to build lifecycle marketing into your own business. For now, it's vital to understand the foundations so you can build on that knowledge later, when we get more specific and technical. Lifecycle marketing describes the points in the customer's or prospect's journey where you:

- Claim their attention.
- Bring them into your sphere of influence (micro-conversion).
- Convert them into a registered and/or paying customer (macro-conversion).
- Keep them as a customer (retention).
- Turn them into a company advocate (loyalty).

Of course, along the way many individual customer lifecycles are cut short by abandonment and attrition, which is an unfortunate reality of the fickleness of the marketplace. You can, of course, drastically reduce this attrition by keeping your customers engaged.

Let's take a closer look at each stage, although we'll save the deep dive into each—including case studies—for a little later.

Attract: Turn Their Heads

Target

The first part of the Attract phase is all about understanding your target customer clearly. There will be distinct groups of people within your target audience, called segments. Each segment is different, so you must target them differently.

If you understand clearly exactly who's in the segments within your audience, you'll be able to talk to people like individuals, and do it in a way that pleases them.

Attract Interest

Once you're clear on your audience and its segments, you'll have some understanding of what makes them tick. When you understand them, you'll become clear on their wants and needs. Using that information, you can start to put together valuable content and offers to attract their interest: lead magnets.

This stage is often called awareness: the point at which a buyer first learns about your brand or product. You'll now be aware of where they hang out, both online and offline, so you can meet them where they are and tell them how they can get hold of the valuable content and offers you're creating. In other words: you can advertise and distribute content.

Collect Leads

Advertising and driving traffic to your website are worth nothing if you don't have a mechanism to automate collecting lead information. Lead magnets are a way to offer an ethical bribe to encourage someone to give you their personal information in exchange for valuable content and offers.

We collect this information using sign-up forms. Your lead simply puts their contact information into the form. (These examples may sound simplistic, but they are incredibly simple strategies at their core, which is what makes them so powerful.)

This trade-off of someone's contact information for something of high value to them gives you something crucial: permission. Permission marketing allows you to contact a person when you want. But you still need to gain the most vital ingredient: trust.

Engage: Win Their Trust

Educate/Nurture

Once you have someone's contact information and permission to contact them, your main focus is to build trust. Your entire aim as a marketer is to build a relationship with your prospects and customers. If you're in this for the long haul to gain loyal customers who advocate you and your business every chance they get, you have to build a relationship with your audience.

The foundation of successful relationships is a win-win environment of trust. You provide value, they exchange money for more value, and you build the relationship thus. If at any point the trust fails, the money will cease along with it. Your erstwhile customer will take their business elsewhere.

If you want to add value, customers need to understand the value they're receiving. Which means you must educate your audience. This is usually a relatively straightforward process as your contact has signed up to receive an item of value to them, and now you can educate them on that information.

Education doesn't just involve giving information away; it also involves satisfying specific points along the customer journey. There are specific emotional markers to help you build and develop your relationship and move your prospect along their awareness path.

This educate/nurture phase, together with the next phase—adding value—are the two most vital stages in the entire lifecycle. Without them, you'll never reach your potential within your business. Engagement is all about the relationship, and it's where a buyer will become interested in your product or service.

Add Value

Education is nothing without value. While education will move customers along their awareness and sophistication paths, and further down the funnel, it must go hand in hand with value. The world today is simply too busy and too noisy for you to keep someone's attention if you do not provide value. You need to give value to get value.

Value isn't just required when you first start building a relationship with a potential customer; it's vital if you want to continue the relationship. You must continue to provide value for as long as you want the relationship to continue. And if happy customers with long and substantial customer lifetime values is what you want, you must focus your attention on education and adding value.

Sell: Get The 'Yes'

Offer

Once you've established a relationship and added value, your prospects will be primed for purchase. Now you can make the offer. Make sure your offer is consistent with the original problem your prospect signed up to solve, and make sure your prospect understands the benefits of what you're offering: how you'll help solve their problem and the relief they'll feel when you do.

If you build and structure your offer effectively, you'll avoid buyer's remorse, prevent refunds, and create genuine excitement and desire for your products. There are many proven methods you can use to help ensure people say 'yes' to your offer, the best of which we will cover in the **Sell** deep-dive.

Close

Unfortunately, no matter how well-crafted your offer is, a proportion of prospects simply won't take you up on it. This is where the **Close** process comes into its own.

In the **Close** section, you focus on getting those prospects who are on the fence firmly off it. A subset of your prospects will be interested enough to view your offer and visit the shopping cart, but may not be committed enough to buy. This is known as 'abandonment'.

To avoid abandonment, focus on the pain your prospect may currently be feeling, how your offer will help them solve that pain, then explain the benefits they'll enjoy once they buy from you. If you have not built a relationship and fostered trust, your prospects will not convert to customers. They simply won't trust you enough to do so.

During the **Close** phase, you'll want to focus strongly on any objections your prospects may have to buying from you. If you acknowledge their objections and put to bed any niggles causing people to hesitate, you'll touch all the points you need to make a sale more likely. The **Sell** phase comprises **Offer** and **Sell**—which is the decision part of the customer awareness journey.

Wow: Knock Their Socks Off

Deliver and Wow

After purchase, you have an opportunity to build a **Wow** experience and go above and beyond to keep your customers engaged. This is where you focus on turning a customer into an advocate, by knocking their socks off.

One of the easiest ways to do this is to add value after the point of sale. Providing a continual nurture after-sale encourages your customer to actually use your product or service, and assures them you weren't just after their money. This is how you continue to build trust and engagement.

After a little time has passed, check in with your customer to see how they're doing—this continued engagement will help them feel you care about their success. If your customer is overjoyed, you know you've done a good job and they are on their way to becoming an advocate for your business. If they're upset, this is your opportunity to fix the problem before you lose their custom completely and, in doing so, gain yourself an advocate.

Some of the more advanced marketing models have a stage for this called **retention/loyalty**. This is described by Marketo as 'when a customer purchases the product, uses it, and keeps coming back'[4]. But I believe this oversimplifies the role you need to play in keeping your customers engaged after the point of purchase.

Offer More

I like the way Marketo thinks about this stage as 'growth: when you identify complementary products to cross-sell or up-sell the customer

---

4 Marketo, *The 5 Principles of Engagement Marketing* https://uk.marketo.com/ebooks/elements-of-engagement-marketing/

to continue to provide increased value'[5]. Immediate up-sells aside, when you're sure your customer is satisfied, it's time to move them along their journey by offering them more. This is, of course, an up-sell in the traditional sense—but you can also cross-sell here if you don't have an obvious progression.

The art of a successful up-sell or cross-sell is to accelerate the desired outcome, i.e. fix the current problem faster. But don't just focus on selling more—focus on continuing to provide increased value. If you don't do that, you can kiss your customer lifetime value goodbye!

This is exactly why the **offer more** stage comes after **deliver** and **Wow**—not before. Your customer must engage with and trust their purchase before they'll consider buying more from you. If you provide increased value in the **deliver** and **Wow** phases, your customer retention will create a good customer lifetime value.

Referrals & Testimonials

This is often referred to as '**advocacy**: When customers love the product so much that they influence others to consider the product as well'.

It's a good idea to ask for customer testimonials after each purchase. But be careful when you ask. Your customer needs enough time to consume your product to properly answer—but not so long they can't remember! Make sure your customers are happy before you ask for a testimonial, because if they're not happy and you haven't done anything to fix it yet, you risk upsetting them even more. Net Promoter Result scores are a great way of testing the water before you ask for a testimonial, and they identify the unhappy customers you need to reach out to. Then, of course, come the referrals. It's not always appropriate to ask for a referral, and you must be careful what you do with the information you get from the referee. Some countries (Canada, the EU, and the UK, for example) have very strict laws on data protection. More on this later.

Lifecycle Marketing: Real Life

Let's take a look at the *Attract-Engage-Sell-Wow* model in real life, with real people, and a real company—morphing theory to practice.

---

5 Marketo, *The 5 Principles of Engagement Marketing*

Cleancorp

Taking a company from $1.2m to $3.75m in turnover is no small feat. Doing it with only eight members of staff and 241 customers is something else entirely. By focusing on each part of the lifecycle marketing framework, and continually and systematically implementing systems and campaigns with Infusionsoft by Keap, Cleancorp did all this and more, winning Lisa and Hamish MacQueen the coveted title of Small Business Icon for 2013.

Cleancorp is a leader in the facilities and cleaning industry in Australia and New Zealand, thanks to their relentless focus on strategy. It's a service provider, and its customers are fiercely loyal because they focus on helping to provide a healthier and more productive workspace for every single client. Let's break down their strategy and successes within the lifecycle marketing framework.

Attract

By combining SEO, pay-per-click adverts, and lumpy mail strategies (the art of sending physical gifts in the mail), Cleancorp has managed to rank as number one for the most important keywords in their industry. Their most successful lead generator is their blog, attracting large volumes of traffic to the website. The company has done particularly well in adding strong calls to action on the webpages.

Lisa correctly identified that no one contacts and browses a cleaning company out of curiosity: generally they have a pressing problem, and they need to solve it as soon as possible.

Understanding the target customer and being able to anticipate what they're most interested in means Cleancorp can get the most effective lead magnets in front of them to attract their attention and collect information. Two of their top performing lead magnets are a free report called *Eight mistakes every office manager should avoid* and a fantastic piece of lumpy mail.

The lumpy mail contains a UV light torch. It's a powerful black-light torch that shows up all sorts of dirt and grime. This is genius, because leads receive the torch, switch off the lights, and discover exactly what their current cleaning company is missing—and why they need Cleancorp. I love this lead generator, and Cleancorp's prospects do too.

The company is also active on social media—it makes sure it's where the audience is.

Engage

Once Cleancorp's prospects have opted in, or asked for a quote, they're immediately segmented by what they've registered interest in. This ensures they only receiving nurturing information that's super-relevant. Initially, leads are segmented by what they want, e.g. ongoing commercial cleaning, one-off cleaning, carpet cleaning, etc. Next, they're segmented by geographical location, number of services per week, and so on. Then the highly targeted nurturing begins. Prospects receive online and offline communications, as well as courtesy calls. They receive UV light torches, cleaning books, value-add emails, sales emails, information emails, testimonials, and all kinds of marketing materials, all of which builds rapport, adds credibility, provides value, and builds Cleancorp's brand.

Crucially, the engagement doesn't stop when people become customers. Customers go through an on-boarding process and a nurture series designed to build trust and promote Cleancorp's mission, to 'keep the cleaning enterprise clean'. Cleancorp's continual focus on engagement means their leads and customers feel cared for and engaged all the way through the buying process.

Sell

During the sell phase, Cleancorp rocks its industry with its conversion rate, which sits at around 40 per cent. Interestingly, some of their best leads come from engagement sequences. These are people who were interested but did not convert at first. Rather than chucking them out as duff leads, Cleancorp nurtures these people with quality content.

Once someone fills out a quote on their website or calls in via telephone, the on-boarding process kicks in. First, the lead is segmented by the size of the job. If it's a small job, an onsite quote is unnecessary and the team completes a form containing the pricing details, which cleaner will do the job, the profitability, cost to the customer per month and per week. As soon as the employee hits the submit button, Infusionsoft by Keap emails a detailed quote to the prospect.

If it's a big job an onsite visit is necessary, which is where Cleancorp's automation is truly stellar. After the prospect gets in touch, Cleancorp completes a form with the date and time they'll meet. If it's more than three days away, the prospect gets a follow-up message. Hamish receives a detailed notification of when and where he's going, who he's meeting, and a link to the quote form he needs to complete during the onsite meeting.

Once onsite, Hamish asks questions and, using his iPad, he completes the form as he's being shown around. At the end, he hits the submit button and an email goes off to the prospective customer he's just seen, thanking them for their time and promising to send their quote soon. The office gets notified that a quote needs completing, they assess the information, fill out a quote-completion form, and the customer gets their detailed and personalised quote.

As soon as the new customer says 'yes', a welcome email goes out, the accounts department is notified to complete financials, and a cleaner is assigned and sent the information about the new job. Customers and cleaners even get their contract straight away—all automatically via email. The key is, it's not just sales that are automated, but the workflow behind them, too. This creates a completely streamlined yet customised experience for the new customer.

Wow

After the point of sale, Cleancorp realised it had problem keeping customers, so they devised a great bit of engagement to keep clients for longer. Initially, they addressed the problem by focusing on more training and supervision of their staff. However, this didn't help—complaints remained high and their retention rate was poor.

Cleancorp soon realised the main issue was a disconnect between the customer and the onsite cleaners. The customer didn't really know the cleaners, so couldn't develop a relationship with them, which meant they didn't really care about them. It's easy to fob off a faceless service for someone cheaper—even if that more expensive but faceless service does a great job. Instead, Cleancorp focused on humanising the relationship between the cleaners and the customers.

Now, as soon as a new customer is confirmed and contracts are signed, Cleancorp's special new-customer welcome campaign kicks in. It's full of personal touches: new customers get a physical welcome card from their new cleaner. The card isn't just any old standard thing— it's from the person who'll be in their office every day, keeping their world clean. The card has a photo of the cleaner and a little information about who they are and what they like to do. Putting a human face on the service has brought complaints down, shot referrals up, and created happier cleaners and happier customers.

Then Cleancorp moves onto **Wow**. Two weeks after contracts are signed, Hamish—the managing director—sends out cookies and a thank-you card. And—you guessed it—this is all automated.

But how does a cleaning company go about up-selling in the next phase of lifecycle automation? Every campaign has a specific up-sell built into it. Customers like having something extra done every now and then, and there are also seasonal campaigns for the holidays.

Now for referrals. Thirty per cent of Cleancorp's customer base comes solely from referrals. That's no fluke—it's because the company is more passionate about good service than about money. This attitude breeds customers who are happy to refer others when appropriate. To capitalise on this they ask during onsite visits, but they also have a campaign designed to ask for a testimonial and a referral. If they get a referral, Cleancorp rewards the customer and the cleaner with a $25 gift card. All of these phases combined lead to a very satisfied customer base. Over 90 per cent of Cleancorp's customers are happy with their service, which is an excellent score in their industry.

Cleancorp achieved all this success by intentionally designing campaigns and automation for every part of their customer journey. They brought human behaviour into the mix and made the workload scalable through automation with Infusionsoft by Keap.

While their customer satisfaction speaks for itself, let's take a look at the numbers. Since designing and implementing these processes, Cleancorp has grown from 120 customers and sales of $1.2m, with an average yearly customer value of $10,229 to 241 customers and sales of more than $3.4m, with an average yearly customer value of $14,252.

That's a year-on-year growth of 64 per cent. It's phenomenal. And you could do it too. Here's why.

Lifecycle Marketing: The Science & The Data

As I said in the introduction to lifecycle marketing, humans go through specific steps to buy stuff. The awareness journey I mentioned is actually based on a much more complicated system put together by researchers and psychologists over many years.

In fancy terms, this is called the purchasing process, but I prefer calling it the buying system, which is how we'll refer to it from now on.

Marketers have taken this buying information and made it far more accessible but, at the same time, most of its potency in the understanding of why we do what we do has been lost.

We're going to fix that. You and I are going to break down the science behind buying systems so you can see exactly why you need a good lifecycle marketing strategy. This system is based partly on how we make decisions, but there's so much more to this than the decision-making process. A general buying system follows a path combining self-actualisation, base human needs, societal influence, learning processes, life stages, socio-economic forces, and more.

Basically, we humans are nothing but a complicated and connected mess. Luckily, we've been studying this mess called behaviour for many, many years. The general buying system is most often referred to as having eight parts[6]:

- ↓ Need/Want Recognition
- ↓ Information Search
- ↓ Evaluate Alternatives
- ↓ Purchase Intentions/Decision
- ↓ Purchase
- ↓ Product Use/Evaluation
- ↓ Disposal Action
- ↓ New Needs/Wants

Let's take a look at each of these.

---

6 Bennett, A. (2010) *The Big Book of Marketing*. McGraw-Hill Education

Need/Want Recognition

There are several common needs and wants that motivate humans to do stuff. These needs start at the most basic biological necessities (yes, those we share with all the animals) and progress towards wanting inner happiness.

As it stands, there are two main (accepted) models of needs and wants: Maslow's hierarchical model[7] and Mowen's simultaneous model[8]. Maslow's five-stage model is by far the most commonly known, and its pyramid-like structure is forever seared into any psychology student's brain. The model is laid out in a progressive manner, meaning the base needs must be met before the next need can be addressed and satisfied. It's generally purported that you will never reach the top of the pyramid, but you'll always try to get there.

The needs and wants are:

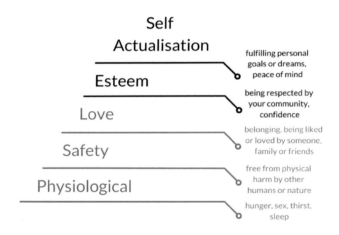

From the bottom, Stages 1 to 3 can be considered to be needs, and

7 Maslow, A. H. (1968). *Toward a Psychology of Being*. New York: D. Van Nostrand Company.
8 Mowen, J. (1999) *The 3M Model of Motivation and Personality: Theory and Empirical Applications to Consumer Behavior*. Springer

Stages 4 and 5 are wants. The theory is you're always motivated to satisfy these needs and wants, and so you'll buy products or services to help you get there faster.

Advertising globally is particularly fascinating. Richer countries and communities are discernible from their poorer, less fortunate, and less-developed buddies merely by the levels of needs and wants the advertising panders to. Watch adverts in any developed country and you'll notice they focus on Stages 4 and 5: pure wants. In less-developed and poorer countries most advertising hovers between Stages 1 and 3.

In first-world and developed societies, the pyramid is inverted. Stage 1 is of little concern to most people, because basic needs are met almost as a given. Stage 2 is slightly more important, and so on—until you get to the largest area of demand: Stage 5, because these societies are consumers. Those in developed countries always want more to achieve self-actualisation. So the needs are few, but the wants are many. Less-developed societies don't have that luxury. Their basic needs must be met first.

But let's examine a slightly different school of thought. Mowen's simultaneous model of needs and wants differs mainly in that his research indicates safety needs and self-actualisation needs can happen at the same time. I like this model, as I feel it certainly fits first-world societies—but I don't believe it accurately portrays us as a species across developmental ranges.

Both these models demonstrate that you need to know where your audience is at. If you're a bustling start-up in a backwards small town, you may not find the chic target audience you're looking for. Be clear in the target phase about where your audience is from a societal-development perspective. Identify where your audience is and be clear on what they need and want, and how you fit into that. Which matches neatly with the target phase of lifecycle marketing. Basically, all the money in the world is worth nothing if you're dying of thirst and you can't buy water.

Desperately Seeking Information

Once you've identified the need/want, you must have information in order to satisfy it. We can't make any kind of decision without some information, and the entire industry of content marketing helps satisfy this stage. There are three parts to this section:

Amount Of Information

Factors such as the level of involvement with the product, the importance of the purchase, price, complexity, the habit of using the product, and the consequences of making a poor choice all affect how much information people need.

The higher the stakes, the more information is required. Ensure you're providing the appropriate amount of information for the consideration taking place. Make sure that you're diligent about what your audience expects to receive, so you can match and exceed the information level required, positively.

Sources Of Information

When looking for information, we automatically search our own information resources first. This is an internal search of our memories, and it's based largely on whether an experience was good or bad. This is why it's so important to ensure consumers have positive associations with your services, products, and brand. You want people to recall you quickly and positively.

If the internal search comes back incomplete, uncertain, or empty, consumers do an external search for information. They may reach for their phones, ask a friend, read a magazine or book, or even a wander up and down the aisles of a store.

Whichever way the search happens, you want to control as much of it as possible with good, handy information and positive word of mouth. This is often referred to as brand equity—the amount of mental real estate your brand holds.

This used to be the realm of the big boys because success came down to big advertising bucks and who could get the biggest billboard, newspaper space, or prime-time TV slot. Not so anymore. With a good attract-and-engage strategy, you can now move quickly and with more personality than the big boys can. Thank you, internet!

The Learning Process

Learning is the process of gaining information and understanding it, through experience or study. Which is exactly what you're doing right now. When I refer to learning in this book, I mean thinking about how someone will go about finding and understanding the information you're giving them to help them make their purchase decision. The model of learning developed by WJ McGuire is the most common model used:

↓ Stimuli.

↓ Exposure.

↓ Attention.

↓ Comprehension.

↓ Perception.

↓ Acceptance.

↓ Retention.

↓ Memory.

This is fascinating because most marketing planning fails to take the first five phases into consideration. Most businesses jump right in with the assumption that the message will be understood, accepted, and retained. Job done.

But we need to identify where to put the stimuli so the right audience sees it. Then we must make sure the audience receives the right amount of exposure to retain the information. And finally, we need to craft something that captures attention.

On top of all of that, it misses out perception completely. It's your job to make sure your services, products, and brand are perceived in the correct way. You do all this by deeply understanding your target audience, what they're interested in, and what they're looking for.

Evaluate Alternatives

When customers have gathered all the information they can, they weigh everything up. Ultimately, they choose the option that gives them the biggest reward; the option that best satisfies their needs or wants. This choice will be affected by their existing beliefs and attitudes (internal influences) and their societal or group norms (external influences). Here is your opportunity to let your engagement shine. Pre-empt questions and contrast yourself with your competitors to make the decision easy for your potential customers. Educate all the way!

Purchasing Intentions/Decision

If you know where someone intends to go, and they're lost but you know the area well, you can help them plan the best route possible to get to their desired destination. This is a good analogy for what you can do for your customers.

By finding out your customers' intentions you can tailor their journey. By segmenting your audience based on their interests, you can make sure you give them the best possible experience and information. This is value-add and nurture at it's very best. Then, when you've provided what they need, step in and ask for the sale.

In today's digital world we signal our purchase intentions clearly by what we search for, and how we search for it. A good SEO strategy, some decent retargeting, and good nurturing will put you miles ahead of the pack.

The Purchase Act

Slippery transactions are the best transactions. It's painful handling money over, so don't make the hardest part of the journey even harder by putting barriers in the way of consumers handing over their hard-earned cash. Make the transaction as easy as possible. It needs to be quick and simple. No waiting in a line, doing too many clicks or—heaven forbid—actually having to pick up the phone. Hell no.

Slipperiness is what we call online processes that need to be smooth and frictionless. Payment in any form needs to be incredibly easy. Streamline where you can, automate to avoid human error—whatever you do, make it easy.

Once you've made the payment process as simple as possible, don't ask for the sale once then hide. Watch purchase intent closely, so you can help any stragglers who aren't quite sure over the line.

Product Use/Evaluation

When a consumer buys something, life gets binary. They're either happy, or they're not. This is your next big research point. When your customer has their long-awaited 'thing' in their hands, what comes next? Are they overjoyed? Disappointed? Confused? Overwhelmed? Underwhelmed? That's all up to you.

This is your after-care point. Your **deliver** and **Wow**. It's called that for a reason; it's your turn to build the relationship by being dependably awesome. This moment will be stored in your customer's memory and recalled at a later date. Is that recall going to be positive or negative?

Your marketing after the sale is vital to helping validate a consumer purchase. It's crucial to get them using the product as soon as possible. Help your customer avoid buyer's remorse or post-purchase dissonance. You're in this for the long haul, not just because it's profitable to do so, but because you should give a damn about your customer base and your reputation. Help them want to stay.

Disposal Action

What will your new consumers do when they've finished with what they just purchased?

Disposal actions originally referred to throwing away packaging and being conscious of that part of the product consumption. However, this term now refers to businesses throwing their customers away just when they're ready to spend more money. This is your up-sell, cross-sell, and down-sell opportunity. Identify the next step in the journey for them... and make it happen.

New Needs/Wants

After identifying the next step in their journey, look at their new needs and wants. At Automation Ninjas, we call this 'avatar progression'. It's the point at which you've solved a specific problem for your customer, so now something else is the main problem. Your customer has moved on to the next part of their needs and wants hierarchy. This is where you start their journey again. It's time to help attract them on to the next phase of your offering and move them through the lifecycle again, but for a different product.

Summing Up

These are the eight stages of the buyer system. Some are more complicated than others, but each phase holds its own importance in creating a happy customer base that actually uses what it buys.

It's evident from each of these stages that you need to have a plan in place, and you need to make sure you're being deliberate about where you want to take your consumer at each level.

Your end goal is to build a strong relationship through adding value for your customers. Do this, and people will recall you appropriately with positive connections, and you'll have happy customers. This requires a framework, and lifecycle marketing provides that framework.

So, let's start building that plan of yours. In the next chapter we'll take a deep dive into **Attract**.

The Brain Hack

There's a vast amount of information available at our fingertips, and more ways than ever to consume it. We fracture our attention. Consumers are distracted and their brains are lazy.

System 1 filters out everything that isn't immediately and obviously useful. It often makes bad choices, preferring the immediate reward over the logical one. This can lead to bad buying decisions, and regretting our purchases.

If we regret our purchases or have bad experiences finding information, we're left with a negative emotional marker for the company we have bought from.

Hack Your Buyer's Brain

If you want to hack your buyer's brain, don't allow it to make poor decisions and create negative associations with your brand. Take advantage of the learning process and awareness journey:

1. **Attract** your buyer's interest by finding out what they want and need.

2. **Engage** them with useful and valuable information that helps them make their decisions.

3. **Sell** to them by making offers consistent with their problem and overcome any objections they may have to buying.

4. **Wow** them with a slick payment process and delightful after-sales campaign that solves any problems and makes the customer feel valued.

CHAPTER 3: Attract—Turn Their Heads

"It requires wisdom to understand wisdom: the music is nothing if the audience is deaf."

~ Walter Lippmann

CHAPTER 3: Attract—Turn Their Heads

Attract: The Principle & The Problem

When a tree falls in a forest and there's no one around to hear it, does it make a sound? There are two ways to answer this paradox—through physics, and through philosophy.

If you pay attention to quantum superposition, the answer is an undisputed yes. And no. At the same time. Which, of course, doesn't help anything. Philosophy approaches the puzzle from another direction: hearing sound is perception, so from that camp it's a hard no. This does raise an interesting question, though. If no-one's there to hear the sound, can it be considered sound? In the same vein, if no-one's paying attention to your business, does your business really exist?

Arguably the biggest battle you face today is the attention battle. How do you go about getting the attention of your desired audience? Going back to our philosophical outcome—if your potential audience pays you no attention, you don't exist to them. If your audience doesn't know you're there, it's not possible for them to buy from you. So before battling conversion rates and employing all the little tactics that go with it, you need to nail your attention strategies. Because without attention, you have nothing. Let's talk attention. And, specifically, let's talk about how you attract attention and hold attention.

Let's talk about the first phase of the lifecycle marketing journey and how it will help you overcome the challenge of getting people to notice you. The **Attract** phase of the lifecycle marketing journey is all about getting attention, keeping it, then converting it, so you can move onto the next phase—which is building the relationship.

We'll start with a super piece of research done by good old Google. Back in 2011, Google commissioned a study into how consumers make decisions about what products to buy[1]. As we have more choice available now than ever before, Google wanted to know exactly what we do to help us make decisions about which products to purchase.

The original three-step mental model of marketing Google was researching consisted of the following journey:

⬇ Stimulus

⬇ See it on a shelf/purchase

⬇ Consumption

Proctor & Gamble coined the phrase 'First Moment of Truth' to refer to the **purchase** point in this journey[2]. This is the point at which the consumer first sees your product and makes it theirs. The 'Second Moment of Truth' is the **consumption** point, when your consumer actually uses and experiences the product or service they've bought:

⬇ Stimulus

FIRST MOMENT OF TRUTH

⬇ See it on a shelf/purchase

SECOND MOMENT OF TRUTH

⬇ Consumption

---

1 Google (2011) *Winning the Zero Moment of Truth.* https://www.thinkwithgoogle.com/marketing-resources/micro-moments/2011-winning-zmot-ebook/
2 Huang, Y., Hui, S.K., Inman, J.J., & Suher, J.A. (2012) 'Capturing the "first moment of truth": understanding point-of-purchase drivers of unplanned consideration and purchase' *Marketing Science Institute* 12–101

Google discovered around 88 per cent of consumers undertake a huge amount of consideration activity before they buy: a massive research phase. Now, if you work in marketing or are an avid content marketer this will come as no shock to you. But back in 2011, this discovery birthed mass content marketing as we know it.

What really shocked Google was that even for relatively spur-of-the-moment purchase decisions, such as which restaurant to choose, consumers consulted an average of 5.8 different sources to help them make a decision. For bigger decisions, such as buying a car, on average consumers consulted 18.2 sources. That's an enormous amount of information being consumed.

This massive research phase was named the 'Zero Moment of Truth' (ZMOT) by Google:

ZERO MOMENT OF TRUTH

↓ Stimulus and research

FIRST MOMENT OF TRUTH

↓ See it on a shelf/purchase

SECOND MOMENT OF TRUTH

↓ Consumption

The Zero Moment of Truth is the point between a consumer first realising they need something and being committed enough to buy it. It's in the ZMOT where your consumer pays attention. Nailing the ZMOT is how you get to capture that sweet attention. No more existential crisis for you. Simple, right? If only...

You must compete with millions of websites, social media platforms, and life in general for your consumer's attention. How, then, do you go about acing the ZMOT?

First, define your target audience as clearly as possible. In order to figure out how to get someone's attention, you need to know who that someone is. When you understand who the person is, you can identify what sort of research they'll do, what sort of questions they'll ask, where they hang out, what they care about, and what they actually want.

At this point it's tempting to go off and create a ton of information about your products and how you can help your customer so you can provide all the information these poor little scamps who are researching away could possibly want.

Your product can help them! This is how!

Stop right there, tiger. You have another problem.

Your audience and prospects don't give a damn about you and your products. At all. Any attempt to dish up, 'Here—look at how awesome this product is, and why' will turn them right off. You see, consumers have learned the smiley, helpful man in a nice suit with the nice teeth and nice hair is actually a salesman who'd eat his own children alive if it meant he could close the next deal. Whether or not this is true (it usually isn't, of course) doesn't enter the equation.

Consumers have been trained not to trust you. Not by themselves, not by some nefarious overlord, but by bad business practice. They've been trained by living through an era where they had no power and the salespeople had it all. The internet has fundamentally changed that power balance.

People don't want to be sold to, but they *do* want the information you have. They want to arm themselves with as much know-how as possible. Welcome to the era of the research-obsessed consumer.

The all-knowing Google produced a few stats on just how obsessive consumers are about information: we check our smartphones an average of 150 times a day[3]. And in any moment of information searching, we turn to a search engine to help find the goods and information we need. That's a lot of searching for the right information.

Now we have an odd juxtaposition. We have consumers arming themselves with all the information they can lay their hands on—yet they're warier and more suspicious of getting into a situation where they believe they might be sold to.

The key to surviving in this strange void is to always keep your ideal customer front of mind. Keep reminding yourself that your plans and their plans are very, very different. They want to make the best choice

---

3 Google (2011) *Winning the Zero Moment of Truth.*

for themselves—you want them to buy something. They don't want to be sold to; they want to choose. You want to sell them something; you want them to choose you.

The easiest way to nail this is to deeply understand your consumer: know them inside and out, identify their mindset at the point of research; then help them achieve their desired outcome. This helps you get attention, add value, and build trust. No scary, shiny, cannibal salesman in sight.

Attract: The Solution

Be Useful

The best strategy to bridge the void is to be as useful as you possibly can. Always remember your ideal customer's agenda is different to yours. Create an environment they actually care about and want to be a part of. Provide information they want to consume, and position yourself as the best source of useful information. Provide value, don't sell.

Let's get super clear on exactly how to do this. This is where the **Attract** phase blossoms. **Attract** starts with target, and target is about being wholly focused on finding the exact audience you can help best, and who will respond most enthusiastically to you and your value.

Demographics & Psychographics

Start with a highly focused and targeted audience. Your first task is to identify exactly whom you're targeting. Enter stage right: demographics.

Demographics refers to specific groups or segments of the population. It's all the rather dry statistical data relating to your desired prospects—facts like age, gender, ethnicity, income, and geographic location, as well as other types of information about who they are, where they live, and what they do.

Demographics are the rough outline of your target audience. These come in handy when you try to figure out where your audience hangs out and what they're up to.

For example, using demographics will help you pinpoint where you need to provide value. Using the data, we can see approximately

79 per cent of online adults use Facebook[4]. Which is fantastic, as you can now firmly say that, yes, your audience is probably hanging out on Facebook. But we can go further. We can see the highest percentage of users on Facebook is in the 18–29 age group, with a giant 88 per cent of all online users in that group using the platform. The more we dig, the more we can see Facebook is (at the time of writing) a decent way to find your target audience, no matter the grouping.

But the astute marketer should ask the question: is Facebook the *right* platform? Perhaps it's too crowded. Perhaps we need a slightly quieter but more targeted platform. What about LinkedIn? Well only 29 per cent of adults who are online use it. But on digging deeper, we can see if you're looking for educated professionals with a relatively high income, LinkedIn is perfect.

Demographics give you a pretty cool understanding of what platforms your audience hangs out on, allowing you to separate your desired audience from the rest of the planet.

However, the problem with demographics is they're superficial; they lack vital information. My favourite example of how this problem manifests is a parable based on real data.

Let's suppose a luxury car company targets a specific audience. The criteria for its ideal customer are as follows:

→ Male aged 65–70

→ Based in or around London (showroom location)

→ Married

→ Has adult children (so will spend on himself)

→ Wealthy, with high income

→ Enjoys high-performance cars and luxury

→ Supports charities and causes (will be swayed by company's charitable work)

→ Travels and enjoys the finer things while travelling (especially the mode of transport)

---

4   Pew Research, 2016: http://www.pewinternet.org/2016/11/11/social-media-update-2016/

All this makes it much easier to create an effective advert to sway the consumer, which is exactly what our imaginary car company has done. Through their targeting, they identified two people who fit their criteria. Here are their demographics:

➔ Male, born in 1948

➔ Spends a lot of time in and around London

➔ On his second marriage

➔ Two children

➔ Successful and wealthy, self-employed with disposable income

➔ Loves dogs and high-performance cars

➔ Enjoys travelling, sports, fine wine

➔ Likes to holiday in the Alps

➔ Indulges in music, has a soft spot for charities

These are real people. Super-defined people, right? We know so much about them! But you wouldn't want to show them the same advert, because although they might buy the same car it will be for different reasons, so different adverts will appeal to each of them.

That's because the two men the imaginary luxury car company has identified are the Prince of Wales and the Prince of Darkness: Prince Charles and Ozzy Osbourne. And yes, the parallels between the two are quite startling, and very real, much to my great amusement.

This presents a real issue in business, as most customer profiles are created *only* from demographic information. But the demographics don't give us any information about what people might like, which groups they may be members of, or anything relating to what motivates them. The demographics have left out the human element: the part that makes us tick and gives us our personality.

Understanding the human element allows you to provide real value. Enter stage left: psychographics. Psychographics help explain and define the *why* behind buying behaviour. This is the gold dust. While demographics may help you segment your audience at a high level, psychographics help you understand what's important to your prospects, identifying their desires and motivations. And that's how you get attention. The double whammy of demographics and psychographics allows you to tap into the ZMOT.

The combination of good demographics and clear psychographics is beautiful to behold. Knowing what motivates your audience, and precisely where they may hang out, means you can talk to them appropriately. You get clarity on their attitudes and interests and, therefore, on how to drive engagement. In particular, your psychographics help you design the environment you create with precise and intentional communication.

In other words, in this crazy, research-obsessed world it's crucial to be explicit about what sort of information you need to provide, where to provide it, and how to present it. To get started, ask yourself:

- What interests my audience?
- What's their attitude to their problem? Or the solution?
- What opinions might they hold?

These starting questions are IAO variables: Interest, Attitude and Opinions. The way you communicate with consumers needs to align with those variables. When you look at the IAO variables of our two princes, two very different personalities emerge, giving you the foundations for a human connection. Demographics alone couldn't cut it. Now we're clear on who we're targeting, we can move on to identify how we can attract their interest. This is the second part of the **Attract** phase.

Attract Interest

When you understand what your prospects care about, you can put together information and adverts that appeal to them—but you still need to add value. Otherwise you're just that creepy salesman again. This is the real heavy lifting of the **Attract** phase. To add value, define and plan the following:

- Problem
- Mindset
- Outcome

- Awareness level
- Trigger
- Micro-moment

It all starts with a problem. One of the best exercises you can do for your business is write a long list of the problems you solve for your customers. This list sets out who you are for your audience. Your marketing activities should reflect that. Once you're clear on the problem you're solving, it's time to step into your audience's shoes.

With their problem in mind, what's their current mindset? What are they feeling about this issue? Are they hiding? Are they overwhelmed? Scared? Lost? Confused? Identifying their mindset allows you to choose the best way to talk to them about it. Their mindset dictates what you say and how you say it. For example, if your prospect is eager to solve their problem, providing them with the best ways to solve it may well sway them. But if they're confused about their problem, you need to help them gain clarity before you introduce the how-to.

When considering mindset, what's your prospect's desired outcome? What do they actually want to achieve by solving the problem? There are always two levels. The immediate outcome is what will happen *right now* if they solve their problem. Then there's a longer-term outcome, one that taps into their life goals. If we look at the outcomes for some of the reasons people get marketing automation, invariably the short-term outcome is to get organised, save time, and convert more leads. But the longer-term outcome is quality of life, particularly for smaller business owners who want to reduce stress and enhance quality time. This makes for quite powerful messaging.

Now for awareness level. At this stage you're clear on who your ideal customer is. You know what problems they're experiencing, you understand their frame of mind and what outcomes they want to achieve—but you also need to know where they are on the awareness journey so your messages are relevant.

All the way back in 1966, Eugene Schwartz proposed five levels of customer awareness which he published in his book *Breakthrough Advertising*[5]:

---

5   Schwartz, E. (2004) *Breakthrough Advertising*. www.breakthroughadvertisingbook. com.

1. The most aware: your prospect knows your product, and only needs to know 'the deal'.

2. Product-aware: your prospect knows what you sell but isn't sure it's right for them.

3. Solution-aware: your prospect knows the result he wants but not that your product provides it.

4. Problem-aware: your prospect senses he has a problem but doesn't know there's a solution.

5. Completely unaware: no knowledge of anything except, perhaps, his own identity or opinion.

This is all well and good, except the levels Schwartz proposed are product-focused. They were proposed at a time when the market was considered a 'seller's market', meaning the shiny cannibal salesmen had the upper hand—you just had to get ahead of your competition.

We currently live in a buyer's market, so we must turn the list on its head and look at it from a prospect's point of view. Here are the exact same levels, but with your prospect and their problems as the focus point:

1. The most aware: your prospect knows your solution, they know how it relates to them and how it will solve their problem, and they only need to know how to make the purchase and solve the pain now. They want to know what the best deal is.

2. Product-aware: your prospect knows you have a solution, but not how you fit in with their problem specifically. They're not sure you can solve their pain and problem.

3. Solution-aware: your prospect knows the outcome they want, they know there are solutions out there, they're researching, but they don't know *you* provide the solution.

4. Problem-aware: your prospect senses they have a problem and the pain is there, but they don't know there's a solution. They're starting to research their pain.

5. Completely unaware: your prospect has no knowledge of their pain. Something isn't right, but they can't put their finger on what it is.

It's a subtle change, but it's immensely powerful as you shift the focus from yourself to your customer.

When you understand your prospect's awareness level, you can provide specific content to cater to their level, helping them progress through the awareness levels and approach the point of purchase. Start figuring out where your audience is by asking: 'What does my prospect already know?'

Now you can get clarity on what type of information they might be searching for and how in-depth your information needs to be. As a pleasing consequence, you'll discover how you can add value to their research journey.

To help with relevancy, it's useful to identify what may have triggered the problem in the first place and build out from there. Triggers make us turn to a search engine for help. Unsurprisingly, Google has dominated the research on this, too. Google refers to these triggers as micro-moments.

Knowing the context of the micro-moment helps you clarify whether or not your content will be of use, and therefore valuable to your prospect, at that point. If it's not valuable, they'll move on. If it is, you get a foot in the door to start building trust through the value you provide. When you think of what may have caused your prospect to start searching, ask yourself, 'What are they doing in this moment?'

For example, let's imagine a company selling DIY tools wants to get its audience's attention. It knows the biggest research point will be the price, but it's also aware there's more to the consumer's journey. Long before the customer looks for the price of a specific tool, they may research how to do something and what tools they'll need for the job. This is the company's opportunity to provide value. If the audience searches for 'How to hang a door quickly', the company can create valuable content on how to do that, tell the consumer what tools are required, and explain why theirs are the best choice. Thinking about the trigger and micro-moment here is essential.

The DIY company's consumers are looking for information on how to do this because they have a problem: they need to put a door up, fast. They don't have time to mess about with long-form eBooks or hour-long videos. They need something quick and consumable, like a step-by-step list they can refer to as they go along, or a short video.

After the customer has hung the door, there are myriad other topics the company can help out with—like how to look after the door and other related topics. This way the company has clearly identified the micro-moment and added immense value for the customer. The relationship is now well on its way.

With all these points in mind, your audience has taken shape and has human context. You know what your audience is interested in, and what will capture their attention. Now it's time to create something to help you build a relationship with them and convert them from stranger to hot prospect. It's time for the third part of the **Attract** phase: collect leads.

Collect Leads

How do you know the right time to ask your audience to convert? I'm not talking about a purchase here, I mean when do you ask for their contact information so you can continue the relationship in a different way. This is where you take someone from anonymity to your database. Most businesses do this with a lead magnet—a juicy piece of content your prospect desperately wants and is willing to exchange their precious contact information for.

Lead magnets allow you to build your relationship—they allow you talk to your prospect a little more in-depth, so you begin to build trust. According to the model we've all been told to use, ideally you exchange a valuable piece of information for their contact information, then you start to sell.

But if you've been following so far, you'll know your prospects aren't stupid, they don't trust you, and they certainly don't want to be sold to. Not to mention that your 'valuable' piece of information is probably available for free somewhere else, where they *don't* have to give their contact information away. So why bother? Why ask for their information at all? You can easily follow people around the internet and communicate solely with retargeting if you're clever about it. But there are a few problems with that.

One issue is ad blockers: they will thwart you almost immediately. Apps and plug-ins allowing people to remain unpestered in their browsing time are becoming commonplace. But the major issue is the one that ad blockers and fast-forwarding ads hint at—people don't want to be interrupted all the time. People want to do what they want to do, without you popping up and bothering them.

So instead, you must focus on being wanted. You want people to want to hear from you. You want people to be interested in receiving your communication. You want them to want to give you their contact information. And you want to do it in a controlled manner. Getting people into your database allows you to do exactly that. Lead magnets are, therefore, still a great option; you just need to let go of selling. Instead, shift your focus to building desire for your products and services.

Knowing exactly when to offer a lead magnet takes investigative work. Ask yourself questions like:

- What questions am I answering here, and how do they relate to my products?
- How far along the awareness journey is my prospect?
- Do I have something valuable enough to ask for their contact information?
- Can I provide the right information at this point to move them onto the next step of the journey?

And, of course:

- How much does my audience trust me at this point?

Getting ahead today is not only about being a better provider; it's about building relationships and trust. It's about the customer experience from start to finish. That begins with getting their attention, then takes teeny little baby steps towards gaining enough trust to convince them to swap their contact details for more information.

It is possible to get people to give you their name and email address if you have something they absolutely need *before* they trust you—but the problem with this is you haven't earned the right to continue the relationship, so their attention wanes after they get what they want.

A method with far more impact and longevity is to build the relationship through micro-conversions: progressively building trust and engagement. In 2001, Bryan Eisenberg first wrote about micro-conversions as the incremental actions people take in order to complete the end goal—the purchase[6].

Since then, the online conversion communities have used the term to talk about the actions a user takes on a site that increase their chance of buying something—actions such as visiting pricing pages or adding items to a cart. We can use the same principles to build relationships.

The concept of micro-conversions will help you hack relationship building. When you look at a customer lifecycle you can see each stage someone goes through is an action point. These action points are when your prospect chooses to make a positive engagement with you: they clicked on your ad; they filled out your lead magnet form; they opened your emails; they purchased your products. They made a decision to take an action with you.

This is similar to the process we use to build relationships as humans. If you ask someone to marry you the first time they meet you, chances are they'll say no. (And probably run away fast.) If you ask them on the first date, they'll probably still say no—but the odds have improved. Go on fifty dates, and you'll have a substantially better chance of getting a yes.

Your prospects are no different. Don't ask them to buy the first time you meet them; build the relationship and up the stakes incrementally. First, simply get them to click through to your content. That's one micro-conversion. Then reward them with awesome content. Don't ask them to marry you then—you've only just met them!

Rather, up the ante and get them to commit a little more by asking for a date. This could be another piece of content, or a lead magnet. Now they're getting to know you. Up the ante again. Each time they say yes, you get a micro-conversion.

If they say no, give them a lower commitment—like another piece of content—until they trust you enough to invite you into their wallet.

Micro-conversions help you win over suspicious consumers. Consumers who have no trust. Micro-conversions help you build that trust, incrementally. But don't just stop with your prospects, use micro-conversions with your customers, too. Do it for your existing list. Use it as positive training.

---

6 Eisenberg, B. (2011) 'Optimizing the conversion rate optimization process' https://www.bryaneisenberg.com/optimizing-the-conversion-rate-optimization-process/

Micro-conversions help you create positive rule sets, which means your list pays active attention to you. This is healthy in a way that interruption advertising can never be.

The best way to use this strategy is to enable the person who is ready to commit *and* provide options for those who aren't quite there yet. With every micro-conversion you level someone up and take them further along their journey.

By now, you've identified your target audience, you know what interests them, and you're focusing on adding value around that. That gets you attention. Once you have attention, get your prospects to micro-convert into a more controlled environment where you can continue to build a relationship with them. As we'll discuss in the next chapter, if you don't build a relationship with them, you're just educating someone else's customers. Now let's look at what goes into a good lead magnet.

Lead Magnets

A lead magnet's role is to move your audience along their buyer journey by building the relationship through trust. When your prospect gives you their contact information, don't ruin their trust by selling at them. Rather, reward their trust with a value-first approach.

Make sure your lead magnet concept is right for their awareness level, then ensure the information includes at least one micro-conversion or call to action to help them move to the next awareness level.

Here's what makes a good lead magnet:
- Solves a real problem.
- Promises and provides a quick win.
- Super specific.
- Quick to digest.
- High value.
- Instantly accessible.
- Demonstrates your expertise/unique selling point.

If you have any lead magnets out at the moment, review them to check they cover each of the points on that list. Remember their purpose is to move your audience along their journey from stranger to buyer—not necessarily to sell to them. A lead magnet that covers all of the above points will help you get and keep attention.

Attract: Real Life

With all that in mind, let's look at a business that's done exceptionally well at nailing the **Attract** phase.

Lamar Tyler New Media

In December 2007, a young couple started the website BlackandMarriedwithKids.com. The Tylers, a married couple, were sick of the insidious negative image and perception of African-American marriage in society and the media. To combat this negativity, they wanted to focus on positive messages about marriage and relationships. They wanted to actively promote and equip marriages within their community.

To do this, Tyler New Media offers a range of products to help strengthen marriages. This includes ebooks, audiobooks, films, home-based study systems, and my personal favourite—a membership site that connects couples in need of help with therapists and coach-led training sessions. They even offer cruises!

This is a clearly defined target audience if ever I've seen one. The Tylers knew exactly whose attention they were interested in attracting, and they knew why. Using their blog, they built up a strong following, and in 2009 released their first documentary film. The blog attracts large volumes of traffic because it's focused on the issues African-American couples face, and it talks directly to those couples.

But the Tylers knew a popular blog wasn't enough to allow them to rest on their laurels. They needed a strategy to attract new visitors, capture the readers, and turn them into subscribers and customers. So they focused their **Attract** strategy where their audience hangs out—social media.

Let's look at how Tyler New Media (TNM) has built a 400,000-strong following on Facebook alone, and a list of 119,000 email subscribers.

First, TNM uses relationship articles to drive traffic back to their website. They do this by sharing and posting the blogs on social platforms (Twitter, Facebook, Instagram, and Pinterest), as well as advertising to custom and lookalike audiences and pairing up with other brands. TNM focuses on reaching out to its community, not selling.

Once TNM has attention and gets the click through to the website, it uses a plethora of ways to funnel people into lead magnets: sidebar sign ups, pop ups, banner ads, and strong calls to action. They may also drive traffic straight to a landing page.

The primary lead magnet TNM uses is something the audience wants—a free four-part video series on how to create unbreakable relationships. Critically, they don't always drive ad traffic straight to the landing page. Rather, they build trust and engagement through other content first. They drive people to relationship articles and sprinkle their website with calls to action so when the prospect is ready they can make the choice to engage.

Segmentation is a priority and is done based on interest, with clearly defined lead magnets enabling them to identify and create that segmentation. The video series is about marriage, but TNM also offers free ebooks and webinars for singles and couples, attracting prospects who'll be primed to buy when they do find themselves getting married.

Once a prospect has signed up, segmentation and attention are still a priority to ensure TNM stays top of the prospect's mind. Content is distributed heavily across their social networks to encourage engagement and repeat interactions with the brand, and is also sent to their list to continue to nurture and engage with prospects.

TNM offers email-based challenges to people to help them achieve quick wins and improvement their relationships. Tyler New Media continually provides relevant and useful information through their blog, webinars, and social interactions to show their audience how much they really care and demonstrate how much they understand where they are right now. They do an excellent job: the TNM audience really feels understood.

With their continual commitment to a niche and their specific audience, Tyler New Media has evidently targeted well, captured attention, and understands clearly what is of interest to their audience now, and what will continue to be of interest in the future. By doing this, they've grown their social following to over half a million fans.

Their list has grown from 9,000 to 119,262 people (an increase of 1,200 per cent), and directly correlated to that is their revenue, up from $75,000 to $500,000—a growth of 566 per cent. Phenomenal.

Attract: The Science & The Data

As we adapt to new technology and the internet, we incorporate it more into our lives. The more we integrate new ways of doing things, the more our behaviour online becomes commonplace, which allows us to interweave it in our social structures.

New behaviour becomes normal, and because it's normal and comfortable all the biases and inconsistencies that make us human come out and we behave normally. This means that because the internet and social media have become an integral part of our lives, we behave the same way online as we do offline; we carry over our biases and inconsistencies from 'real life' to online interactions. We make the same mistakes online that we do offline, and we look for the same social cues online that we look for offline.

Keith Ferazzi had a great one liner which perfectly describes this. He said: 'We're moving from the Information Age to the Relation Age'[7].

Gone are the days when consumers were simply looking for good quality information. Now, they're looking for helpful information laid out in a way that relates to them, which is written and created by people and businesses they like.

The consumer's focus is on forming informational relationships. Humans tend to develop and build relationships by familiar association, meaning we choose to associate with people who are similar to us.

We socialise with groups who like and dislike the same things we do, and who think the same way. This has serious consequences when it comes to political polarisation, gender and race discrimination, and so on—and we unfortunately have our evolution as a species to thank for this. This is no excuse for being an a-hole—but we can at the very least explain it.

7   Clark, D. (2014) 'Networking In The Internet Era: An Interview With Keith Ferrazzi', *Forbes.*

We evolved as a social species, and our evolutionary advantage was not only our individual intelligence, but also our group intelligence. In the squishy bit we call our brain lie the amygdala and the mesolimbic system. The interaction of these two areas controls what we see as community. Our brains are always looking for community, because community enhances our chances of survival. While that may not be true in the same way in the 21st century, it has been true for most of our evolution—for millions of years.

Looking at how these two areas of the brain govern us, we know the amygdala is responsible for a range of emotional reactions linked to danger (among other responsibilities), while the mesolimbic system deals more with rewards and positive associations with things that help us survive successfully[8].

Their interaction for community is fascinating. The amygdala generates fear and distrust of things like predators, and cautions us against the unknown. The mesolimbic system releases dopamine to make us feel good and happy about things that help us survive.

However, most of this happens subconsciously, which makes it notoriously difficult to test. Even when we're conscious of discrimination, we're often unwilling to admit it.

Thankfully, a clever group of researchers started Project Implicit in 1999[9]. They use the Implicit Association Test to tease out the unknown and embarrassing biases we carry about people around us. The test measures the attitudes and beliefs people don't know are there, or don't want to talk about—and its results have shown exactly how biased we are.

The amygdala and mesolimbic systems are incredibly black and white in their actions. They allow us to split the world into in-groups and out-groups. In-groups are 'safe' and trigger the reward systems, while out-groups are 'not safe' and trigger fear and distrust. The data collected by Project Implicit backs this up beautifully. The implications of this for society are huge, but as businesses it explains why you need a tightly defined target audience and why you must pander to them.

8   Lieberman, M.D. (2007) 'Social Cognitive Neuroscience: A Review of Core Processes', *Annu. Rev. Psychol.* 5(8) 259–89
9   Project Implicit. https://implicit.harvard.edu/implicit/demo/background/thescientists.html

If you're similar to your target audience and they feel you're part of their in-group, they get a dopamine hit from the mesolimbic system, and create a positive association with your company. If your target audience sees you as part of the out-group, they simply won't trust you. If you're ambiguous, you still lose, because you're still not part of the in-group.

A good demonstration of this human desire to be part of an in-group is we still gravitate to easily distinguishable boxes. Apple has succeeded fantastically well at this, and mass forum sites like Reddit and Mumsnet are proof of our birds-of-a-feather nature. Of course, this then means we choose businesses and products we feel best reflect our own beliefs and values to our chosen social circles.

I love that the internet social world is no different from our original ancestral groupings. We all love a good dopamine hit. Thanks, mesolimbic system!

This all sounds completely esoteric right? Not to worry. There are a few simple ways to turn this into a workable output.

In order to appeal to the right consumers, you need to understand what's important to them and reflect that. Ensure your audience feels socially comfortable, which is why the target stage is so vital—it's about understanding your consumer well enough so you can create a place that feels like home to them. Carve out a little slice of the internet where they can associate with people who really *get* them. It's these inbuilt psychological needs that make the target phase work.

First, examine the internal and external influences on your audience. Which segments of the community do they identify with? Once you understand that, you can tailor your messaging for validation and understanding. Good ol' in-group stuff. Internal influences consist of things like life stage, income and spending capacity, and beliefs and attitudes.

Life stage includes both chronological age and where someone is in their life plan. Are they older, retired, with grandchildren? Are they younger, single, and looking for a life partner? Or perhaps still young but married and thinking about having kids? Their age, coupled with their position in their life plan, dictates what they need as a consumer. How do your products and services relate to their needs?

Income and spending capacity dictate what they can spend on those needs. Figure out how that relates to the cost and value of your products or services. It's important to know whether or not you fit within their discretionary income or disposable income.

Disposable income is what your consumers have left after taxes. They'll use that money to pay for necessities like housing and food, as well as savings and luxuries.

Discretionary income is the bit left over after taxes and necessities. Ask yourself if you're a necessity or a luxury. How does that relate to what your target consumer has to spend?

Life stage and income are often included in demographics. They're pulled out of the statistical data of the population. However, they only get you so far. They won't get you into the in-group. This information gets you a rough outline, but now you need to look to psychographics to get to the in-group.

Psychographics are what make us human, and they consist of the beliefs groups hold, what they value, and their attitudes and opinions. As we discussed earlier, interest, attitude, and opinion variables are incredibly important. What are the IAO variables for your audience? Further to that—what do they value? What does the in-group really care about? Is it freedom and justice? Vegan food? Capitalism? Shooting guns and drinking beer? Or saving the planet and drinking gin? Don't stop there though—what are their beliefs? Do this exercise both in a broad sense and related to your products or services.

Beliefs are an emotional acceptance of a concept or an idea. For example, stereotypical Apple users believe their product is superior, whereas stereotypical Android users believe the opposite—that Apple users are sheep. These strongly held beliefs impact buying behaviour, so it's important we understand them.

You can go even further by looking at your audience's new-product adoption patterns. Are they innovators and early adopters? The majority? Or laggards?

Then look at their shopping attitudes. Are they elite shoppers? Will they always buy the most expensive or luxurious item they can afford? Or are they strategic shoppers? Will they always do the research to figure out the very best option? Perhaps value shoppers, always buying the cheapest option? All this information allows you to firmly identify your target audience, which allows you to understand how to break into their in-group.

From here we move onto attract interest. Simply identifying the in-group isn't enough—you also need to capture their attention. Remember, consumers are looking for an informational relationship. They still need the information. Most importantly, consumers are loyal to their *need* in the moment, not a brand.

Sixty-five per cent of people look for the most relevant information (that fits their needs) regardless of the brand. Which is awesome if you want to break into the market, but awful if you're trying to hold your audience's attention.

This is why is it so important for us to create content for our consumers, rather than just adverts. And this is where data from Google comes alive:

1 in 3 consumers have purchased from a brand or company other than the one they intended because of the information provided in the moment they needed it.[10]

Knowing how to provide the right information is half the battle. You can start by asking yourself, 'Does my consumer know they have a problem?' The answer will enable you to pinpoint where your customer is in their awareness journey, as we touched on earlier. It also helps you provide the correct information for what they need in the moment.

Google then suggests a three-pronged approach to optimise where you spend your time, and how. They recommend three areas of focus: be there, be useful, be quick.

Be there. Anticipate micro-moments then commit to being there and helping when those moments arise. Understand when your consumer will look for information. Is it when they're just about to do something? When they're actively doing it? When they're planning on doing it?

What they're doing when they start looking for something dictates the information they engage with. This moment of intent is what

---

10   Google (2011) *Winning the Zero Moment of Truth.*

Google refers to as a micro-moment.

Be useful. Be relevant to needs and give your consumers the answers to the questions they're asking. Google is all about relevancy, and Google is only ever all about something if the consumer is all about it. Consumers expect that when they turn to Google for information they will find relevant answers to their questions. If they don't, they get frustrated. Google doesn't want frustrated searchers. It wants the consumer to keep coming back and finding the information they want and need. It's vital to keep this in mind when you create content—keep the consumer happy with relevancy and utility.

Be quick. Make finding information easy and frictionless. Look at Google's recent mobile data: there's been a 20 per cent increase in mobile sessions, but an 18 per cent decrease in the amount of time spent per session. Be fast if you want to capture attention. You can't mess around proving to your consumer that you're in the in-group— they need to feel it immediately. Talk the talk, walk the walk, and look the look.

You may be wondering how you actually measure up to all this. The best way to test this is with a 'share of intent' metric. That is, how many times are you there as a fraction of all category-relevant searches? Seventy-three per cent of consumers say regular, useful information is the most important attribute when selecting a brand.

Then, of course, when you *do* show up, how relevant, useful, and impactful are you? Don't forget, your consumers are not shopping and making decisions in a vacuum where you're the only choice, so it's important to know how you stack up against your competition.

In essence, you're looking to add value, build a relationship, and provide a solution. To do that you must have your consumers' best interests at heart, and you cannot do that without clearly understanding them.

Spend time finding and closing the gaps, add value, build informational relationships, and dominate your in-group. Prove you're not the shiny cannibal salesman. Prove you care, and prove you are worthy of people's trust.

That is how you get and keep attention in a culture of fractured attention and massive distrust.

The Brain Hack

Our brains decide who to trust and not to trust based on whether or not they're in our 'in groups'. If your brand isn't on your target market's 'safe' list, they won't trust you—and they won't buy from you.

Our inherent biases and prejudices can cause many social problems, but our brains evolved that way to keep us alive. If you want to get around those human biases, you need to...

Hack Your Buyer's Brain

You can hack your buyer's brain by doing three simple things:

1. **Target**: Clarify your audience by using demographics and psychographics. Tap into interests, attitudes, and opinions to become part of their in-group.

2. **Attract interest**: Using their awareness level, provide what your customers will find useful, when they want it. Give people what they're searching for.

3. **Collect leads**: Reward your audience with lead magnets that add value and are useful and informative.

CHAPTER 4: Engage—I Am, Because We Are

"Ubuntu."

Nguni Bantu term meaning: I am, because we are.

CHAPTER 4: Engage—I Am, Because We Are

Engage: The Principle & The Problem

We often hear how nurture, trust, and relationships are important in marketing—but no one really talks about why. Bizarrely, the answer to why it's so important and how you can best go about it comes from our evolution as a species and a popularised, yet stolen, phrase from a tribe in Africa. Let's take a look, shall we?

Ubuntu is not only an open source operating system; it's a term with origins in southern Africa. *Ubuntu* is an enduring notion from the Nguni Bantu, and has become somewhat of a popular term among hippies (bless their colourful organic cotton socks), hipsters, and businesses that want to appear 'heart-centred'.

Unfortunately, the term isn't taken to heart as often as it is quoted. *Ubuntu* is a powerful concept, and while the popular translation is, 'I am because we are' the direct translation is 'humanity'. At its cultural core is the understanding that we are all connected by our humanity— we are all the same because we're human, and so we should treat one another with the love and respect humanity deserves. That would be amazing, but it somewhat gets in the way of most businesses' profits.

Which is a shame, as the concept is almost directly linked to said profits.

The amazing Desmond Tutu has a wonderful interpretation of *Ubuntu*. He said an individual's measure of *Ubuntu* is through their relationships with other people. In other words, the measurement of your humanity as a person is in how you treat the people you have relationships with. This begs the question: 'Where does this fit in business in the 21st century?' Obviously relationships have an incredibly important role to play in our personal lives—we can't survive without them—but what about marketing and business?

We've evolved to rely on relationships. As an evolving species we had an edge because we clustered in numbers. This led to us developing as a social species, and everything that sets us apart from the rest of the food chain is because of this interpersonal connection capability. Our growth in intelligence is linked to how we've evolved socially through sharing the responsibility of caring for our children, sharing resources, skill-sets, and eventually knowledge. Tens of thousands of years of social evolution have brought us to the point where we can articulate through fancy words and terms, 'Yes, we should maybe be nice to each other to survive.' But funnily enough, we've been doing it all along—albeit with varying degrees of success.

However, as businesses continue to evolve, profit margins and efficiencies pushed relationships to the side. What happens to businesses that don't prioritise our innate need for relationships? In a marketplace where businesses hold the power in the consumer–business relationship they survive for a short while before fading into obscurity. But in a marketplace where the consumer holds the power, unless the business has a monopoly over the market, those businesses fail. And that's thanks to our evolved reliance on relationships.

Relationships are vital to surviving as a business. So, what goes into building a relationship? There are various elements, depending on what kind of relationship you're building. A consumer–business relationship is invariably transactional. You're exchanging goods for their money. Vital to transactional relationships is trust. If consumers don't trust you to provide them with what you promised, they won't give you money.

This simple formula works fine for one transaction, but for ongoing services, or multiple-transaction relationships, another element comes in—compatibility. In other words: do the consumers like you enough to come back? So now we're adding personality into the mix too. Isn't it fantastic working with humans?

Profits and efficiency are important, but you won't have either for long if you don't have consumers who like and trust you. How do you win that trust without having to put monumental manual effort into relationship-building? Interestingly, it's entirely possible to do it more easily by focusing on the consumption experience. This doesn't mean you won't make a profit; in fact, by focusing on building a relationship instead of focusing on profits, you're far more likely to make a higher ROI: 49 per cent of companies say they achieve a higher ROI by focusing on engagement over acquisition.[1]

All this boils down to the fact that you can make more money if you're nice to your consumers. It's *Ubuntu* validated by data: trust and relationships are important, and you need to get consumers to like you. And if you focus on that, you can get more money. This is all great!

But what do consumers think? Well, 86 per cent of consumers are happy and willing to pay more for a better customer experience.[2]

This statistic is a fascinating little golden nugget. The more you think about it, the more interesting it becomes. Why are such a large percentage of consumers willing to pay more for the experience? As we've already explored, experience is an intangible and subjective thing. It doesn't impact the quality of the product, only the price. Surely logic dictates that consumers would want to pay the least amount of money for the same thing regardless of how it feels to purchase and receive it?

Well, as it turns out, no. That's not the case, and it all comes down to relationship. Good experiences make people feel cared for. They make people feel special. Which is exactly what everyone—not just every consumer, but every person on the planet—wants to feel: special. We all want to be unique. Just like everyone else.

Cheap and nasty experiences make people feel anonymous.

1 Econsultancy Digital Marketing Excellence Survey. https://econsultancy.com/reports/internet-statistics-compendium/
2 Rockefeller Corporation (2011) Customer Experience Impact Report. http://www.oracle.com/us/products/applications/cust-exp-impact-report-epss-1560493.pdf

For example, picture yourself taking the bus in an inner city, cattle class. You're just another anonymous commuter, with all the other anonymous commuters. Then imagine the same journey, but this time being driven in a limousine. It's luxurious, it's exclusive. It makes you feel like you're *someone*. You're special. And if you have the means, you'll pay more for that experience. When you get a superior experience you feel validated in your special-ness. While this has fascinating implications for premium pricing, it speaks directly to our innate desire for relationships.

Premium experiences ignite some awesome emotions in every consumer. You know the person providing the experience is doing everything they can to make it exceptional. They care about you, and you're trusting them to make you feel special and cared for. The contract that you have with the service provider is a positive relationship. Within this transaction you have care, trust, and relationship, which is precisely why people will pay more for it. And if consumers are willing to pay more for such an experience when it comes to money changing hands, what does that mean for how desirable a good experience is in the run-up to purchase, too?

The world is immensely noisy, but through providing a meaningful relationship, you can cut through a lot of that noise. The first step is to earn trust. And we do that by engaging. While **Attract** is all about getting attention in the first place, **Engage** is about keeping that attention and building on it.

Here's where you get to develop your relationship and carve out a special place for your business in the minds of your consumers. You can have the best lead magnet in the world, but if you forget about your prospect after you deliver it, you've lost a customer before you ever had them. Instead, relentless focus on a quality experience right from the start can have them coming back for more. Remember, if you're not building trust, you're educating someone else's customer.

To gain trust between attracting attention and making the sale, we focus on crafting a catered experience. You do that by caring for your consumer and helping them through their journey to purchase, every step of the way, by nurturing the consumer, educating them on their journey and adding value. Engagement is all about the value-add, because the value-add and nurture process allows you to build trust, relationships, and positive rule sets. To do all this and scale without becoming overwhelmed, you need quality content.

The internet is made of content. It has the answers to consumers' questions, the cat videos, and 50 million filtered selfies. Content allows you to reach your consumer and give them a taste of who you are and what you're about without actually physically speaking to them, and without the consumer feeling sold to. Content is the bridge between getting a lead and making a sale. It's what allows you to **Engage**.

Engage is the second phase in the lifecycle marketing model. It consists of:

→ Educate/ Nurture → Add Value

Your journey to trusting and strong relationships is a constant cycling between the two stages. It's not a linear 'educate first and add value second' or vice versa—the two go hand in hand constantly. That makes it hard to find the appropriate place to start. What content do you need? What content does the consumer need? What's it supposed to look like? And why is this all such hard work? These are the questions that come to mind here... and luckily there's an easy answer:

What do your consumers want to learn?

Create content around the decisions your consumers need to make. Eighty-two per cent of us turn to our electronic devices when we need to make a decision[3]. That means 82 per cent of us are actively looking for content to help us.

Now, you might want to head off and start creating content to nail relationship building—but whoa there, you have another problem. If you create tonnes of stuff for your consumer without being strategic about it, all you'll do is add more noise to the internet. You'll waste time and money creating content people don't care about. Marketo puts this really well:

Marketing is shifting from talking at people, and focusing on transactions, to engaging with people, building meaningful, life-long, and personalised relationships.[4]

---

3 Google (2011) *Winning the Zero Moment of Truth.*
4 Marketo, *The 5 Principles of Engagement Marketing.*

The crucial part of that sentence is 'life-long personalised relationships'. If you create content with the sole intention of just getting consumers through to the sale, you'll just talk *at* them and fuel their distrust. No trust = no relationship = no customers.

Consumers don't just want your content, they want a relationship with the provider they choose—one that's going to last and be fulfilling. Forrester recently said today's consumers 'distrust and resent one-off campaigns that interrupt or intercept them'[5].

Understand that consumers don't really care about you until you give them a reason to do so. They don't trust you—and won't trust you—until you give them a reason. Remember, they want a meaningful connection, but they'll make you work for it. It's your job to match up to that. This isn't a bad thing, because a long, fulfilling relationship with a consumer means repeat sales. Repeat sales give you awesome customer lifetime value, which means more profit for you.

Thank you, *Ubuntu*.

Engage: The Solution

Start building relationships as soon as possible, and focus on it continually. While **Engage** slots in after **Attract** in the lifecycle marketing model, it's crucial to ensure you thread it all the way through your customer journey. While most of the work you do happens immediately after getting a consumer's attention so you can earn trust, don't stop when you have that trust: build on it.

With all this said, what exactly do you need to do? Luckily, consumer behaviour really helps you out here. Consumers are constantly turning to the internet for immediate help, for both little decision and big decisions. The internet has become our crutch. Over 100 million hours of how-to content was watched in the first three-quarters of 2016 alone[6]. Possibly the very best thing about this is it's trackable. There's so much data out there about what your consumers need help with, and all you need to do is discover what's important to them, then focus on being relentlessly and strategically helpful.

5 Marcyes, L. (2016) 'Onward and Upward: Research-backed Tips to Rise Above the Noise on Social Media', Marketo blog: https://blog.marketo.com/2016/02/research-backed-tips-to-rise-above-the-noise-on-social-media.html
6 Google (2011) *Winning the Zero Moment of Truth*.

Marcus Sheridan wrote a fantastic book about being helpful called *They Ask, You Answer*[7]. In it, he expounds on the value of answering consumer questions strategically.

In saving his swimming pool company during the 2007–08 financial crisis, Marcus identified that consumers just wanted helpful answers to their questions. Because of this discovery, he became relentlessly helpful and not only did they ride out the storm, River Pools became America's most-visited pool company website. We'll talk more about Marcus and his journey a little later.

Google, of course, has now released data about how important this kind of strategy is: consumers are 48 per cent more likely to buy from companies that provide instructional content. That in itself is pretty cool, but quality content also builds trust: 53 per cent of consumers feel more favourable towards companies that provide instructional content[8]. That statistic speaks volumes about what consumers want and need. All you need to do is roll your sleeves up and provide it. In **Attract** you focused on what was important to consumers, but now it's time to focus on all the questions your consumer will have throughout the entire sales process—and provide content to answer those questions. It's helpful *and* strategic. Who said you couldn't have your cake and eat it?

Your consumers use content to help inform decisions anonymously. When they've made up their minds they'll reach out to you—when they're ready. First, though, they'll arm themselves with all the information the internet makes available to them and they'll only reach out to you if they decide you fit their criteria.

Do you allow people to decide whether or not you fit their criteria? Can your prospective customers make their decision *without* your input? Don't wait—help them self-educate and give them everything they need relevant to their stage in the journey. Focus on that and you'll overcome distrust and apathy, without allowing your competition to scoot in and steal their attention.

Being useful helps beat consumer tune-out, too, which happens when consumers don't listen to the information you're providing

---

7 Sheridan, M. (2017) *They Ask, You Answer*. John Wiley & Sons
8 Google (2011) *Winning the Zero Moment of Truth.*

because they feel it either doesn't relate to them or is sales-oriented. You must do more than simply show up: connect people with what they're looking for in those moments by providing real-time relevant information. Here, an ugly objection often rears its head: 'My audience is busy, and I don't think they want all this information.'

Well, good ol' Google can help you settle that concern: 73 per cent of consumers say that regularly getting useful and relevant information from an advertiser is the most important attribute when selecting a brand[9]. Consumers gravitate towards brands with snackable, educational content, not brands pushing the hard sell. And people are 69 per cent more likely to buy from companies who help them easily find answers to their questions[10].

As a business, you add value by helping people figure out where they are in their buying journey and providing the solutions to their problems. You then educate and nurture them through the buying process. Let's look at where to start and how to figure out what content you should provide to be as strategic as possible. Where are your consumers in their journey?

➜ Are they right at the start, just realising they have an issue? This is the called the Top of Funnel, or TOFU for short. No, not the food. Way more fun than that!

➜ Or are they aware of their problem and learning more about it and what solutions are available? This is the middle of the funnel, or MOFU.

➜ Or are they at the end of their journey, ready to choose a solution and just trying to figure out exactly which one is best for them? This is the bottom of the funnel, or BOFU.

TOFU, MOFU, and BOFU are possibly my favourite acronyms in marketing! But seriously, determining where your consumer fits is vital to the type of content you provide to answer their questions. As you create content, tailor the education you offer to these awareness levels.

This segmentation is useful not only for ensuring you provide the right content, but also for helping yourself during the sales process.

9 Google (2011) *Winning the Zero Moment of Truth.*
10 Google (2011) *Winning the Zero Moment of Truth.*

As most consumers trundle along in anonymous mode, it's tough to figure out where they are in their buying journey without asking them. By tracking the content they engage with and opt into, you can identify where they are on their purchasing journey. This means you'll know how far they need to go to conversion, and whether or not they're ready to buy. You're super-sleuthing and providing value at the same time.

Wherever your customers are in their journey, focus on providing the content required to nurture them through to the next level. Talk to their needs, problems, and the solutions available. You'll provide immense value and start building that all-important trust. But be careful to always keep your customer at the heart of everything you do. The content needs to be about *them*, not you. Be very clear about what's in it for them. If you're simply talking about yourself, you're doing it wrong.

At each of these stages of awareness, your consumer will have their own mindset and outcome. Discovering what this is plays a key role in the suitability of your content and ensures you're talking to them about them, and not about yourself (lovely though you may be). Mindset means how your consumer is thinking at a certain point. What are they trying to achieve and why? Align your content with their mindset.

The outcome is what the customer ends up with after consuming your content and reaching the end of each awareness stage. It's the summary, the part that validates where they are now and tells them what to do next. When you educate, you're their guide. Help them identify what they *need* to do to achieve what they *want* to do.

Having nailed what you should be doing, and where to start, let's look at each of the TOFU, MOFU and BOFU stages:

TOFU

In the top-of-funnel stage your consumer discovers and learns. They may have some symptoms of a problem and are trying to figure out what it is. Or they may have realised they must do something and they need more information. This is the very first point at which they turn to the internet for help.

Generally, their mindset is: 'I need to know more about this issue' or 'I need to validate the problem'. And their outcome ranges from: 'I get this. I know what it is and possibly what's causing it' through to: 'There are consequences if I don't solve this' or: 'Other people/businesses like me are addressing it...' and 'I can actually do something here to improve xyz'.

Mostly this stage is about learning. Your customers are figuring out their needs and you can help them do it. Ask yourself: 'What needs does the consumer have?' and 'What is their awareness of those needs?' Then tailor your education accordingly.

Consumers are eager for knowledge in this stage, but they're much less likely to buy anything yet. You can help them see the light at the end of the tunnel by offering soft suggestions for a solution to the problem. Use calls to action encouraging them to consume more information—blogs, email series, videos, and other content perform exceptionally well here. Help troubleshoot their confusion and provide more answers to more questions.

Your aim at this stage is to build trust. Let them get to know you, and by doing that you optimise for brand awareness. Content should educate, entertain, and inspire—while increasing the customer's awareness and moving them on to MOFU.

MOFU

The middle of funnel is all about your consumer learning in a much more focused way. Your consumer already has a little information about their issue and some clue as to what they're looking for. Now they want to validate that issue and ensure they have all the information they need. Their mindset is often focused on finding solutions: 'I want to learn more about the solutions available that will help me / my business.' And: 'I want the best for where I am now / the business is now.' Their outcome is based almost entirely on solutions: 'I know which solutions are best for me', 'I know what I need to explore in more detail' or 'I know what I *don't* want'.

By the end of this stage the consumer is completely aware of the various solutions and focuses on researching priorities. They want to eliminate people and products that can't help and consider all their available options. You can best help here by talking about the problems and solutions they have. Be honest and frank, and let the consumer lean on your expertise in an unbiased way—which is one of the best ways you can build trust.

Focus your content on specific questions by providing guides and taking a deep dive into particular topics. You can help consumers compare and contrast options for elimination, using reviews and comparisons. Content here should be more in-depth for the topics they need clarity on.

As with TOFU, your content in MOFU doesn't just help them, it can help *you* be clear on who they are and what they need. You help them by making sure your content provides the information they're looking for, while you're profiling them. Specifically, segment your leads for budget, authority, needs, and timeline (BANT).

IBM originally coined BANT as a way to help its sales team eliminate leads that were not fit for purpose[11]. If you don't have BANT or you can't prove or identify BANT, you don't have a viable lead.

In other words, if you can't identify whether your consumer has the budget for your product or services, whether they have the authority to make the decision about the purchase, whether they have a need for what you offer, or whether they're close to making a decision, then you have no sale.

The order of the operations to follow is: need, authority, timeline, budget (NABT, but it just doesn't have the same ring, does it?). You can use the different types of MOFU and BOFU content to identify BANT in your leads. By creating various types of in-depth content, you can profile and track your audience based on what they engage with.

Your aim in the middle of the funnel is to build that trust relationship using content that clarifies. You want to be the business that helps the consumer reach their desired outcome. Once you've helped them explore their options, you can move them to the bottom of the funnel.

BOFU

The bottom-of-funnel content is all about choice. The consumer is almost at the decision stage and very aware of their needs; they're

---

11 IBM 'BANT opportunity identification criteria' in *Business Agility solution identification desktop reference guide* www-2000.ibm.com/partnerworld/flashmovies/html_bp_013113/html_bp_013113/bant_opportunity_identification_criteria.html

preparing for purchase or final decision. Here, their mindset is very much: 'I need to look at the details of specific options and find the one for me.' And: 'Which option should I choose?' Their outcome should be: 'I've found the one.' And: 'It's time to decide when to purchase.'

Your job here is to not get in the way. Don't accidentally put barriers up that stop people from making their decision. In other words, ensure you're not offering people the wrong type of content or lead magnet at this stage. Instead, anticipate their next steps towards choosing their solution and prepare content that provides education and help.

The questions they ask and the content they consume will give them away, so track it—always be profiling. Questions such as 'product X vs product Y' or 'best X product' and definitely 'cost of X product' will help you identify how close they are to the sale. These questions will help you evaluate their BANT level, so watch their behaviour closely.

Through all these stages, focus on being the guide the consumer needs to get to their solution. It also helps to cement your relationship if you've been nurturing them in a more private environment (such as an email list). Recap the problems you've solved up to this point or provide summaries of what they've already covered. This is the first point at which you begin to move into the sales process. The rest of the time you're the guide they're so desperately looking for.

You can now start moving the prospect onto the solution with RABs, which are one of my favourite types of content. You can use RABs in lead magnets, videos, blog posts, email series—you name it.

RAB stands for Recognise, Agree, and Believe. This is a technique to get your consumers nodding along with you and will prepare them for the sale. By following the RAB formula you get consumers to do several things:

- Recognise they have a problem, and what that problem is.
- Agree there is a solution and the problem can be solved.
- Believe they can solve it.

While most businesses are pretty good at helping people through Recognise and Agree, they fail at Believe—because instead of acting as the guide who helps the hero succeed, businesses make *themselves* the hero. Your consumer is the hero. Not you. Keep their trust by showing them *they* can solve the problem. It may be easier if you help them, and it is completely fine to say so. But they are the hero in this story, and you are the wise guide helping them succeed.

What I love most about the RAB technique is it makes the choice obvious. Although obvious is a double-edged sword. If you create your content properly it will engage the people who are a good fit for you, which is awesome—but it will also repel those who are not a good fit. That is even more awesome. It means the leads you get, and the customers who come from them, are far more qualified and easier to work with.

So, by making the choice obvious, those who are right for you will convert and those who are not will go somewhere else. And that is a brilliant thing.

Once you've got the consumer to the point of being able to choose, go one step further towards getting the sale by helping your audience understand and identify success factors. These are the factors that mean they've made a good choice and will get the best outcome.

Create content that shows them how to identify the success of X, through doing Y. Case studies and real-life examples are great here, but they're not everything. You also want the consumer to identify what's most valuable to them, and why. At that point, they should be ready to make the decision.

And, of course, here you should make content available that explains what will happen if they choose you, and why, helping the consumer to visualise what it will be like working with you.

Throughout this process, **Engage** will help you do a few things:

- Build trust and strong relationships by providing valuable content.
- Get more people to the point of purchase by taking them on a relevant journey.
- Get better qualified and better quality customers.
- Leverage the power of the internet with consumers who know you and know why you're the right choice, with minimal effort.

You now have an educated consumer who knows and trusts you. One who understands your solution (and why it's better than others) and has been nurtured to the point of being ready to buy. They're clear on their needs and how to achieve what they want, as well as being clear on what success looks like to them.

At this point, you've gained trust and permission to sell to someone. The consumers you have now will stick with you because of what you've helped them do. And that is the power of **Engage**.

Engage: Real Life

Holistic Vet Care is a fantastic example of **Engage** in action. They offer a range of services for pets, from acupuncture, chiropractic care, herbal medicine, pool therapy, and physical therapy, to massage, stem-cell therapy, and hyperbaric oxygen therapy.

Lee and Dr Gary Richter brought the holistic services mentioned above into the veterinary industry after Lee was involved in a head-on collision in 2004 that left her with just a seven per cent chance of walking again. It was during this stressful and painful time that Lee used a combination of holistic services to learn how to walk again.

While recovering, she was surprised to find these services were not available for pets. Knowing how vital acupuncture and physical therapy in water were to her success in learning to walk and for alleviating pain, Lee and Gary combined their love for animals and her experience and launched Holistic Vet Care.

The big problem we pet owners face is knowing what's best for our fur babies. I know this all too well through watching my own fur baby Salem go through chemotherapy. Animals hide pain and illness so well, it's hard to know what's best for them. Lee knew she could help alleviate that fear of the unknown for pet owners. She understands that to help pets live the best life possible they need to be healthy and happy—so their owners need to be armed with the right information to help them make the best decisions for their pets.

As a small business wanting to grow, Holistic Vet Care also needed more than just a few adverts to get pet owners' attention. They couldn't wait passively for people to reach out and request information. Instead, Lee and her team wanted to allay pet owners' fears and provide valuable information that could take consumers from being a stranger who is worried about their pet and the decisions they need to make, to a customer with a healthy and happy pet. To do this, they simply uncovered the issues pet owners were concerned about, identifying what they needed, answering questions, and adding value with advice and health services.

To make this happen they used Infusionsoft by Keap and put out brilliant content to change the lives of pets. In doing so they managed to grow the business from $1.9 million to $3.5 million in turnover—*without* significantly increasing the size of their customer base. Rather, they provide a quality experience that keeps consumers coming back for more. They've achieved excellent customer lifetime value through content and marketing automation.

Their first project was simply a newsletter offering bi-weekly pet-care tips. Following the opt-in for this series, Holistic Vet Care sends a survey to the consumer asking for a little more information. This survey allows Infusionsoft by Keap to segment consumers into groups based on the information they want and what kind of animal they have. So now HVC can segment the content based on the pet, ensuring everyone receives only the content relevant to them—for example, they ensure dog owners only receive information about dogs and cat owners only receive information about cats.

If the pet owner indicates they want to know about a specific problem, e.g. pain management, the system automatically adds them to a pain management email series which educates the pet owner about the various options available for managing their pet's pain. They learn about natural remedies, supplements, and the different types of vet visits that can help.

These email series help the consumer move past their fear of the unknown, while educating and adding value. They build trust through information.

Secondly, Holistic Vet Care learned about its customers when they phoned in or visited. The questions or concerns raised in conversations triggered educational emails on various topics. For instance, if an owner mentioned arthritis, Holistic Vet Care offered information about it through an email series that explains different ways they can help their pet.

They didn't stop there though: HVC created opt-in forms and

Facebook ads leading to the content, giving them leads who were responding to specific information. Knowing what consumers were responding to meant Holistic Vet Care could provide relevant and segmented education and nurture campaigns to add value for these new people. They made opt-in forms for various series, which took them from 700 contacts to 1,800—a 157 per cent increase—as well as taking their sister hospital from 1,800 clients to over 7,000 clients, a phenomenal 288 per cent increase.

Content wasn't limited only to new leads, it's used to benefit every pet. This means the same content could be used as follow-up. For example, if an owner had a pet with a broken foot, HVC could offer to send them follow-up information on that specific issue. Or for a wound that wouldn't heal, they could offer services like hyperbaric oxygen therapy. These options can help in ways other therapies may not, and the focus here has always been on educating owners to better treat patients.

This builds long-term trust incredibly effectively. Holistic Vet Care uses what the consumer signs up for to provide value through education. When HVC doesn't know what consumers are interested in, they ask. When clients have questions, HVC answers and educates.

The results for the surgeries speak for themselves, and HVC has enhanced the lives of tens of thousands of pets through their relentless helpfulness.

This is **Engage** in action.

Engage: The Science & The Data

We've looked at the idea of **Engage**; now lets scrutinise the science behind the concept. When we look for information, we don't just turn to our phones. In fact, a fair bit of activity happens internally when we need to resolve a newly recognised need or want. At the point of realising we have a need to fulfil, we undergo a process called information search.

Carol Kuhlthau first described the information search process in her book, *Seeking Meaning: A Process Approach to Library and Information Services*[12]. She expounds on how we look for meaning

12 Kuhlthau, C.C. (2003) *Seeking Meaning: A Process Approach to Library and*

when we don't have enough information. Since then, behavioural science has taken her theory and built it into the consumer buying process, sneakily dropping the word 'process' to make it fit better. What Kuhlthau uncovered over 20 years of research was that we do specific things when we need to make a decision or learn about something. In order to decide what to do, our brain first figures out what we know. It checks two things:

1. How much information do we currently hold?
2. Where does this information come from?

Then we evaluate and decide whether we need to check outside the brain to help make the decision.

When looking for the amount of information we hold, we think about several variables:

- What involvement have we had with this type of situation previously?
- How often have we made this decision before?
- Is it important?
- What are the consequences of making a bad decision?
- Is the decision complex?
- How much does it cost?

If we're familiar with the situation, the consequences are low-stakes, and it's cheap, then we're confident in our own choice. But if the stakes are high, we have little to no information, and the cost is high, then we might need to get more information.

We always check our own internal information before we look elsewhere, which is the internal search. When we undertake an internal search we look for previous information, but we also look for emotional cues. Do we flag up pleasant or unpleasant experiences? Do we remember specific marketing messages? Remember: our brains are lazy, and we want to recall specific information about a specific brand. For example, if you're thirsty, that's a problem. You're at a vending machine and need to choose a drink. Looking at the range of sodas in the machine, you need to decide between Coca-Cola and the shop's own brand. The amount of information available is high. The decision

Information Services. Libraries Unlimited.

is low-risk and inexpensive. Your internal search says you like Coca-Cola, you've tasted it before, and Coca-Cola makes you happy—so the shop's own-brand didn't stand a chance.

But what about external search? If the consumer is uncertain or doesn't have enough internal information, they'll look elsewhere. They first look to friends and trusted advisers if possible, then they turn to the internet, where they look for the information they need to validate their decision.

After this point in the consumer buying process, people go on to evaluate alternatives, make the purchase decision, then store a memory for future information research. This is, of course, strikingly similar to what we covered in what you should be doing in **Engage**... and that's no coincidence.

Lifecycle marketing incorporates the learning process and the consumer buying process and puts a sales and marketing spin on it. Essentially, this process underpins everything we do to retain information. Social psychologist William McGuire created the most widely accepted model[13], as shown.

↓ Stimuli

↓ Exposure

↓ Attention

↓ Comprehension

↓ Perception

↓ Acceptance

↓ Retention

↓ Memory

For a normal consumer this could look like:

---

13 McGuire, W.J. (1976) 'Some internal psychological factors influencing consumer choice', *Journal of Consumer Research*, 2(4) pp 302–19 https://doi.org/10.1086/208643

➜ Stimulus: thirsty

➜ Exposure: sees Coca-Cola

➜ Attention: looking at the ad on the vending machine

➜ Comprehension/perception: internal search

➜ Acceptance: 'this is a good idea: buy it'

➜ Retention: 'this tastes good, commit that to long-term memory'

➜ Memory: integrate into consumer's belief system

Engage and content creation work because it takes the consumer through each part of the buying journey by being relentlessly helpful.

So for your consumer who's making a more considered decision, you might want the journey to work as follows:

➜ Stimulus: symptoms of a problem

➜ Exposure: performs internal search and realises they need external information

➜ Attention: searches online and your content/ad catches their attention

➜ Comprehension/perception: interpretation of message, 'I like this business, I understand'

➜ Acceptance: 'this content is good, I would be happy to see more'

➜ Retention: 'this experience is good, commit that to long-term memory'

➜ Memory: 'I trust this business'

Now the consumer builds positive connections to your business because of the content you provide. The learning process helps the consumer store you favourably in their long-term memory. So the next time this topic comes up, or the next thing they need more information on—for instance, that next question you anticipated they would have—they now have a positive bias towards you and your business.

Each time someone consumes your content, it adds to their internal information store, and each time they access it, you build more trust. **Engage** and content creation help you positively hack the buyer brain through being strategically helpful. All of which prepares you for the next part of the journey: **Sell**.

The Brain Hack

The brain is lazy—so when we need information, we search our own memory banks first. This is troublesome for business owners because human memories are notoriously unreliable—but it's great for our brains because it takes very little energy.

If there's enough information inside our heads to make a decision, we'll make the decision using that info—even if it's flawed. The trouble is, we attach emotions to our memories, so if a good brand has a bad emotion attached to it, we'll disregard the brand.

Only if we don't have enough information in our memories do we go looking outside ourselves. Then it's up to you to...

Hack Your Buyer's Brain

Make sure everything you put out there for potential customers to find, at every stage of their buying journey, is super helpful and valuable. Make your prospects feel good when they find the information they're looking for. Provide TOFU, MOFU, and BOFU content, and anticipate their next steps.

That way, they'll store your information—together with your brand—in their memories with warm, fuzzy feelings. So when they're looking for more information relating to their problem, they'll associate you with good things—and they'll be more likely to buy from you.

CHAPTER 5: Sell Without Slime

"Humans have a knack for choosing precisely the things that are worst for them."

~ J. K. Rowling

CHAPTER 5: Sell Without Slime

Sell: The Principle & The Problem

How good are you at making decisions? What was the last decision you made? Think about what you've done so far today, whether you're just waking up, on holiday, or going to bed—you'll have made myriad choices. We're so used to making thousands of little decisions daily, we take the ability to choose for granted. Every day we ignore the small things we decide because it's easy to think only of conscious decisions as choices. For instance, when you recall the last decision you made, you probably didn't think turning the page of this book was a decision. Or continuing to read this sentence. Or thinking about the fact that you're reading while you're reading the sentence...!

The reality is, your brain makes hundreds of decisions every second. And while we make considered, conscious choices throughout the day, we make many more unconscious decisions. According to research by Sheena Iyengar, the average American makes approximately 70 conscious decisions every day[1]. That's quite a lot, but when it comes to

1 Iyengar, S. (2011) *The Art of Choosing: The Decisions We Make Every Day of our Lives, What They Say About Us and How We Can Improve Them*. Abacus

measuring how many *unconscious* decisions we make, unfortunately there is no concrete evidence, and currently there's no way to study it.

What we do know is that every time you speak you make choices about the words you use, the tone you convey, and the message you send. When you listen or read you choose to spend cognitive energy interpreting what's being said. Every time you walk you choose your direction, speed, and purpose. Our lives are filled with conscious and unconscious decisions, so it seems odd that we are so terribly, terribly bad at it—and we *are* bad at it.

Unsurprisingly, the harder the task at hand, the harder it becomes to make a decision. We're quite comfortable choosing which pants to wear today, but what about how much of your country's current budget should be apportioned to certain subsets of the emergency services? That's a harder choice, and not one you can make easily. This is, in part, why most democratic societies elect officials to help with the much larger, harder, and more considered decision-making processes. Politicians are effectively our representative decision-makers; it's what they do for a living, and they find it hard to get right too. Then there are juries—randomly assigned representatives of society who choose whether an accused person is guilty or innocent—and in some countries, whether they live or die. It's not an easy decision, so we rely on a group of people to make it.

Decisions and choice are part of the fabric of our society, from the little to the large. And yet we fall prey to making terrible decisions all the time. We often make the easy choice over the logical best choice for us, if the best choice is the hard choice.

When we have a decision to make, we often need help. The purpose of a sales role is to affect the outcome of choice in a positive way. It's an explicit, 'Choose my product over theirs, and here is why.' The function of sales is to help you choose.

However, at some point along the way, that purpose got lost. Sales became a method to trick people into buying things they didn't need, and some pretty slimy tactics sprang up. This was the era of the shiny cannibalistic salesman. Whether or not this view of sales is entirely true is beside the point. The *perception* of sales is that it's trickery—but this is a huge misconception.

Sales has a definitive and useful role and it's vital to the success of all businesses. After all, without the sale you have no customer. But is sales *everything*? No, because consumers hate sales. Let's take a look at why the consumer hates being sold to so much, so we can better align sales and consumer needs again.

Consumers have been put through the wringer by sales. They've been force-fed some pretty yucky tactics and most people see sales in the same way they see Brussels sprouts. Sprouts are considered awful demon vegetables, and if that's the perception of the consumer, then that is the reality of what businesses have to work with. It's the same for sales, so sales is pretty bad.

A dear friend of mine, Paul Tansey, wrote a fantastic opinion piece about the death of sales[2]. In it, he talks about what we want to be when we grow up—and how salesman is not a role kids tend to choose.

Sales has become reviled. It's at the bottom of the distrust pile. Kids choose to be YouTubers and influencers, and they still choose to be astronauts and firemen. But not sales people.

This is an interesting conundrum, because sales is still necessary. It may no longer be the only thing every business relies on, but we still need to close the sale to survive. We can't omit the role of sales— instead, we need to listen to what consumers are saying they dislike about it and focus on keeping the goods parts: the engagement, the relationship building, and the long-term vision.

It is possible to have the good side of sales without the bad. If you put a huge amount of effort into building a relationship, it's your job not to kill that relationship with shoddy sales tactics. If you've got this far with your consumer, don't ruin it with an awful sales experience; help the consumer make a decision and feel good while they do it.

When a consumer gets to the point where they're ready to purchase, they've moved into the choosing part of their journey. You've got their attention, you've got a relationship underway, now it's time to ask for the sale.

This point in the lifecycle marketing framework is inventively called **Sell**. It comprises: Offer → Close

---

2 Tansey, P. (2016) *Grandad, what was a 'Salesperson'?* https://www.linkedin.com/pulse/grandad-what-salesperson-paul-tansey/

Because sales has such a harsh reputation, businesses go one of two ways:

1. They embrace sales aggressively and take a *Wolf of Wall Street*-esque approach. Coffee is for closers!
2. They shy away from sales as much as possible, not wanting to be perceived as 'those people'.

There is, of course, a middle ground to be had between the two and, as is often the case, that's where the solution to our sales problem lies.

The very first step to solving this conundrum is determining when to make the offer. The second issue is: how do you get those who are at the right point in their journey, and are a good fit for your solution, to make the decision and convert, without resorting to salesy shenanigans? The answer to these problems lies in behaviour.

If you've been following, by now your consumers should have consumed information relating to the MOFU and are now ready for BOFU content. Ideally, they will think of or engage with questions relating to the bottom of the funnel. If you want to know whether they're ready for your offer, make sure you know what they're specifically interested in now.

It's vital to also have some BANT content in place so you can help them determine whether or not you're a good fit. Ultimately, the behaviour your prospects display gives you a hint about when to make your offer. Nice and simple.

But first, let's talk about the actual offer, because this is where things tend to go all wobbly. Your offer itself needs to be up to scratch, too.

When you actually make your offer, the way it's presented is vital. The internet is full of advice on how to best package up and speak about your products or services. Mostly the advice relates to features and benefits and focuses on how we need to lead with emotion rather than logic. Businesses tend to lead with features first, the facts about our offers, the nitty-gritty about all the awesome things your product or service does. But the internet tells us to lead with benefits instead. Benefits are the impact the features have on your consumer's life. Benefits explain the why behind your offer, the emotional stuff. There are thousands of articles and opinion pieces about emotions vs logic and how using emotion helps with the sales process. But should we pay attention to such articles? Does this approach really work? Because simple emotion vs logic isn't even the half of it.

Humans didn't evolve to make purchases, we evolved to survive. So to navigate through a modern world, our brain hacks itself. It uses two archaic systems to make modern decisions. We're not the uber-logical beings we like to think we are.

Antonio Damasio did some fascinating research into how emotion is indispensable in the decision-making process[3]. He studied patients with damage to the parts of the brain that deal with emotion, but were still of sound mind, and he found they were incapable of making decisions.

Logic gives us the facts about a situation, but emotion allows us to categorise those facts as good or bad. This is why people often tout using benefits as 'the' way to sell. Emotion is vital, but it's not the only component. The consumer uses both logic *and* emotion to figure out if the decision is right for them. Definitely lead with the benefits of your offer—but back your benefits up with logic: the features.

But that's not the end of it because now your prospect needs to actually make the decision. Here the hacking gets even hackier. To accurately make a decision we weigh whether or not the decision is appropriate. To make the choice, our brain measures the potential reward of the purchase against its cost—only there is no area of the brain dedicated to dealing with cost. There is an area that deals with reward, which is great—but for cost, the brain uses the pain centre to understand it.

Seeing the price of a product triggers the area of the brain that deals with physical and emotional trauma. It doesn't matter how little the cost is, your pain centre is the part of the brain that understands price.

Price = pain.

You can reduce the amount of pain, but you can't get rid of it altogether—the pain will always be there. Rather than trying pointlessly to eliminate the pain of purchase, a better strategy is to increase the reward value. In order for a purchase to occur, the reward must outweigh the pain.

There are two components to our purchase decision. The first

3 Damasio, A. (2006) *Descartes' Error: Emotion, Reason and the Human Brain*. Vintage

is whether the decision itself is good or bad and for that we need emotional context. The second is whether we should actually make that purchase, and to go ahead and buy, we need the reward factor of the purchase to outweigh the pain of purchase.

It is not simply that we should be emotionally led in our approach to laying out the offer, we must be strategic, too.

Think about what happens when you allow yourself to let your emotions take over when you're buying something: when you're emotionally compelled to buy something, but you can't logically justify it, you get buyer's remorse. Buyer's remorse happens when we buy something we shouldn't have bought or when we feel we've been duped into buying something.

It feels like a good and sensible decision when we're riding out the emotional roller-coaster, but when that emotional charge dissipates, we're left with an awful feeling of regret. You do not want your customers to feel that way straight after purchase. You want them to be both emotionally elated *and* logically justified so they're happy with their purchase and come back for more.

Instead of using emotional sales tactics, you can strategically combine emotion and logic by using the stages consumers go through when making a purchase[4]:

↓   Justify

↓   Select

↓   Purchase

First, the consumer justifies why they need something, which is vital if you want them to avoid buyer's remorse—so help them justify their decision with logic as well as emotion. Then they select the option they want and use emotion to decide which is best for them: is it a good or a bad choice? Lastly, they make the purchase decision—does the reward outweigh the pain? Your role is to help them navigate through that minefield. Help them choose correctly. Help them decide. That is both the role and the power of good sales.

4 Bennett, A. (2010) *The Big Book of Marketing*. McGraw-Hill

When you lay out the journey you want to take your customer through, understand your customer needs to feel like they're buying into something, not being sold at. We love buying, we hate being sold to. There are ways you can make the process enjoyable as well as helpful.

First, is the buying process easy? It's terrible to get excited about buying something and getting your card out, only to find it's infuriatingly hard to buy. You have to create accounts and click through 50 times, and before you get to the end of the process you're frustrated and upset. That's the worst possible start to enjoying a product. Look at what your consumers have to do at the actual point of purchase.

This ease of doing something is often called slipperiness. Your consumer should be able to slide through the purchase process like an eel in a mudslide.

We don't only face a perception problem in sales, we also create problems for ourselves as businesses selling something. We don't choose the right time to sell, we don't help consumers through their purchase process, we don't follow-up appropriately, and we don't make the buying process slippery enough. Fortunately, technology provides some amazing resources to help us help our customers a little better, and lifecycle marketing gives us the framework to use that tech. Let's deep-dive into how we make that happen.

Sell: The Solution

Offer

Your first port of call is to make sure you offer your solution at the right time. This is what the offer stage of **Sell** is all about. Here, engagement tracking is going to be your most vital tool. Engagement tracking covers a few different tactics to help you figure out where people are in their journey and we'll cover each of these:

- Leadscoring
- Profiling and segmentation
- Tracking positive and negative behaviour
- 'If this then that' functionality

Leadscoring is a tactic that allows you to score your consumers or 'leads' based on criteria. The basic premise is: as people take specific actions, or engage with specific content, webpages, or other activities, you automatically assign points to them. Effective leadscoring also takes into consideration negative engagements (like reading an article on how to cancel a service) and either deducts points or notifies someone to help. Points should decay after a certain amount of time, keeping the leadscore accurate. Effectively you create your own formula for what you believe is a good prospect.

If you automate your leadscoring effectively you'll be notified or have specific sales campaigns triggered depending on the value or criteria of the score. It's pretty awesome and everyone should do it.

I don't abide with using standardised criteria, because your needs for engagement are different from other businesses' needs. So figure out what activities you believe indicate a good prospect, and build your own formula. Tracking this level of engagement gives you hints about when to make your offer. This tactic goes perfectly with the next one: profiling.

Profiling is not just the domain of *Criminal Minds* or crime dramas: use it within your business to identify the different groups of people in your audience. The definition of profiling is 'the activity of collecting important and useful details about someone or something'[5].

Profiling gets a bad rap sometimes because it's often used incorrectly (like racial profiling in the police force)—but it's an incredibly useful tool for you to use in your business to identify the different types of people within your audience.

The way consumers interact with your content tells you broadly what their job role is, what they're interested in, and how good a customer they might be. That information is super-valuable, so don't let it fall through the cracks.

Start by identifying the profiles you want to know about. I find it most useful to split criteria into groups of what you want and what you don't want, then segment down into the individual types of people you want to do business with. You can then take that information and reverse-engineer it from existing clients who fit those profiles. What did

---

5 Cambridge Dictionary Online https://dictionary.cambridge.org/dictionary/english/profiling

they do? And why? Then use that information with your leadscoring to build an idea of who people are before you ever speak to them. This will save you massive amounts of time and allow you to speak to the right people, appropriately, when they're ready for your offer.

Good segmentation and profiling go much further than simply separating your audience into leads, customers, and repeat customers. If you want to properly predict and analyse your customers' behaviour, be as detailed as possible—which is where customer types come into play. Customer types are profiles that help you develop detailed sub-groupings of customers so you can target your marketing to them precisely. Combine customer types with personalised messaging unique to their persona profile, and you have a winning behavioural marketing strategy.

There are roughly 13 groups you could choose to segment by, and you can profile people into these groups relatively easily. Let's take a look at each of them:

Prospect

Someone who's on your list but has not yet made any kind of purchase or commitment to you. Generally, this is someone who's signed up for something but hasn't engaged with your marketing just yet. They may be brand new to your list, and so are complete strangers to you and your brand. Work hardest on developing a relationship with these unknowns.

Suspect

A contact who fits the profile of current customers. This is an extremely valuable prospect type to track because customers just like them have already bought from you, so you know they're a good fit for your products. They are also incredibly useful for super-targeted advertising, as you can do with Facebook's lookalike audiences.

Leads

Prospects who have performed a small conversion, such as signing up to your blog, and have given you some personal information in the process. They've completed some of the small steps prospects take towards the primary goal: conversion. They are engaging with you and doing all the little things consumers do to get to the point where they're ready to become a customer.

New Customer

This is a contact who's just made their first purchase or macro-conversion. Macro-conversions are your end goal (most often the purchase). Tracking and engaging new customers and welcoming them in a unique way can guarantee a second sale and a loyal customer.

New customers are defined as someone who's bought from you a certain amount of time ago, for example 30 to 60 days, depending on your sales cycle. After that time, they're not new. I advocate running specific welcome campaigns just for new customers to help **Wow** them and get a second sale (more on that in Chapter 6).

Active Customer

Customers who've made one or more purchases from you and are currently active are 'active customers'.

Novice Customer

These people are in the process of implementing the product and/or getting training for the first time. Customers in this category often fall into other categories at the same time. These customers differ from new customers because they may already be repeat purchasers (perhaps they've bought more than one of your products or services) but they're new to the product or service they've just purchased. Here, a little hand-holding or extra 'how to' information can go a long way to creating engagement and an advocate customer.

Repeat Customer

These are your ideal customers—those who've made more than one purchase and are buying happily at their expected purchase frequency—in other words, perfect!

Loyal Customer

Each business should have its own definition of what a loyal customer is. Edward Gotham from Ometrica offers this guideline:

"I like to say loyal customers are those that have completed more than three transactions, have been a customer for more than 6 months and have performed a transaction in the last x months. The x months should be relevant to your average sales cycle."

At-risk Customer

These customers have passed your average time period for their next purchase, based on the average purchase rate for other repeat customers, or those in their segment who are similar. Ideally, at-risk customers will re-engage before they become lapsed customers. Careful application of re-engagement strategies can turn at-risk customers into advocates.

Lapsed Customer

This is a customer who has gone far beyond the time they were expected to make their next purchase. Defining lapse rates can be difficult, but a good ballpark is twice as long as your average purchase recency and frequency. A good re-engagement strategy can help rekindle these customers.

Unhappy Customer

These are your upset or angry customers. And although they are your most at-risk customers—and often the loudest—they present your biggest opportunity. Good customer service can help you appease these customers.

If you can fix the issue, and really wow them, you can often turn unhappy customers into advocates by proving you care about them as individuals.

Referring Customer

A happy customer who's willing to refer you to friends and family or provide a glowing testimonial is known as a 'referring customer'.

Company Advocate

An ecstatic customer who wants to tell anyone and everyone about you at any chance is a company advocate. Advocates are your most profitable segment, because they're often your most loyal customers and will bring more customers through the door at every opportunity. You want every customer to become an advocate!

Treat each type of customer appropriately for maximum customer satisfaction. They're all different, doing different things, so treat them differently. Be personable, and make sure you use their profile to offer the right product for them at the right time.

New-customer offers can turn those new consumers into repeat customers—but they're not appropriate for your advocates. You can afford to spend a little more money on keeping an advocate delighted with your service, but you wouldn't do that with every lead because their value to you is unknown as yet.

Your customers are all special: treat them as such.

Now let's look at how you can identify these segments, and how you can best leadscore people. One of the easiest things to help you profile, segment, and leadscore your prospects is to track for two things: positive and negative behaviour. Positive behaviour is what you want to see: visits to your sales pages or pricing pages. People engaging with the content you send them. All the good stuff that indicates you have a hot prospect who's interested and willing to find out more.

Negative behaviour is the opposite of that: abandoning sales pages, not opening or clicking through from emails, looking at cancellation pages or refund information. It's just as powerful to look at negative behaviour, because it tells you if you're going to lose a sale before you've even made it—or that someone simply isn't interested so you don't waste time on them.

Tracking these behaviours helps you leadscore; looking for patterns helps you profile and segment people.

Your job isn't done when you know what your audience is engaging with, though. Knowing what they're doing and how they're profiled is useful in and of itself, but you can use this information even more wisely. Use it to plan your 'if this then that' strategy.

Use the information you collect to move people on to the next stage of their journey. So if someone engages with X content, then offer them Y content. If they take action X, then suggest action Y—or have your team do action Y.

Leadscoring, profiling, behaviour tracking, and 'if this then that' functionality allows you to create super-personalised journeys. This is segmentation in practice. Do all this and you can offer people the right thing at the right time and reap the benefits.

Companies that experienced 360 per cent higher conversions from personalised content could only do so due to segmentation[6]. That's pretty awesome—and it's the power of offer exemplified. That's what you want to be doing.

But what if you don't bother? Well, 74 per cent of consumers are frustrated if their journey isn't personalised[7]. You do not want to be known for a shoddy journey. So segment, track, and profile for readiness and fit—then make the offer.

Now you've made the perfect offer, at the right time, and you're fairly certain you've offered the right product for what your prospect needs based on their engagement. Job done, right?

Not quite so fast, amigo.

If you're not comfortable with sales, it's easy to fall at the last hurdle. Once you've made your offer do your due diligence and ask for the close. Consumers often face decision paralysis (also known as analysis paralysis). You've probably experienced it yourself: when you have so many options to choose from you struggle to decide, and end up doing nothing at all.

Consumers want to make the best choice possible, and in doing so will research as much as they can. This, of course, throws up myriad options, and you'll only be one of them. While you've done everything you can to help them make the best choice, you can't account for what your competition gets up to.

What you *can* count on here is you won't be only one in the running. So now you must focus on getting them to choose, positioning yourself as the appropriate choice, and enabling money or contracts to change

6 Google (2011) *Winning the Zero Moment of Truth.*
7 Google (2011) *Winning the Zero Moment of Truth.*

hands. This is the Close part of the **Sell** phase.

Even though your entire focus so far has been getting the consumer to choose, they'll still do some final justification about their choice. How do you go about getting the decision?

By now, it should come as no surprise that content plays a major role. Through content, you can break through their decision paralysis and help them decide. Ask yourself a few strategic questions to help define what really matters at this point. Your job is then to cover these important considerations and help solidify their choice.

Start with: 'How will they define success?' When you know what a successful choice looks like to the consumer you can validate it with an in-depth recap of your offer, or even with final case studies, reviews, and comparisons.

Then ask: 'What is most valuable?' What's the one specific thing your customer is most hoping for? Help them see how their choice will help them achieve their desired outcome.

Then look at their highest priority. Will your solution help them achieve it? Tailor your content to what they want to get out of this decision and help them see how you differ from the other choices available to them.

Clarity about what your customer will achieve, and differentiation from your competition, are the keys to helping people overcome decision paralysis.

Be honest in this process—don't just talk to their desires and wants. Talk to their objections, too. If you explain common objections and set out reasons your product might not be right for them, you'll help your prospect makes the right choice (even if it's not you).

Honesty allows you to dig into the relationship you're building and demonstrate a level of understanding most businesses won't display. Ask yourself or your sales team the following questions: 'What do they ask for during the buying process?', 'What types of sources do they trust?' and, most importantly, 'Why *wouldn't* they buy from us?'

Your answers to these questions once again act as proof points that you're the right choice, but just as powerfully, they act as proof points that you are *not* the right choice for consumers who aren't a good fit.

Helping consumers who are not right for your offer to understand that will save both them and you a lot of pain and hassle in the long run.

With these questions answered, and your offer made, you've helped the consumer justify and make their choice. All that's left for them to do is purchase.

Now they've chosen, they're just looking for the best deal or outcome. They'll clarify their last concerns and then make it happen. The phrase 'getting the best deal' often makes businesses think they need to offer a bargain or a discount. However, lowering your price is rarely the right solution.

Look back at the original formula for purchase intent. When a consumer is going to buy, their brain works out the fit of purchase as follows:

$$Net\ value = Reward - Cost$$

By clarifying objections, leading with emotion, and backing up with logic, by differentiating and contrasting your offer, you will do a good job of showing the reward value. Simply dropping your prices now could do more damage than good because it could devalue your product or service.

Premium brands often offer the exact same product as lower-priced brands, but at a higher price. *Which?* magazine provided an intriguing example involving cars[8].

Consumers are willing to pay an additional $31,000 for the same car with different branding. The Aston Martin Cygnet and the Toyota IQ are the exact same car. They are both made by Toyota, and the only appreciable differences are cosmetic. The Toyota IQ sells for $17,000 and the Aston Martin Cygnet sells for $45,000 plus. The average price discrepancy is $31,000.

Consumers were quite happy to pay the additional amount because of Aston Martin's brand reputation. Interestingly, the Cygnet is no longer manufactured and has now become a cult collectors' item. The irony that the IQ is still being made and is still the same is almost painful.

8 www.which.co.uk/reviews/new-and-used-cars/toyota-iq-20082014, https://www. autocar.co.uk/car-news/new-cars/saying-goodbye-aston-martin-cygnet, http:// under-the-skin.org.uk/news_aston_martin_cygnet.html

This is just one example of brands nailing their focus on increasing the perceived reward instead of decreasing the perceived cost.

You must decide how your pricing positions your brand. Focus on increasing your net value, not decreasing cost.

Making Buying Slippery

You've made the offer, and your focus on the close is laser-like, so don't let the process of buying kill the sale: make sure it's as streamlined as possible. Lean on conversion-rate optimisation to help you make the process slippery and frictionless, speeding up conversions. It should be as easy and pleasurable as possible for consumers to give you money.

Look at your buying process and ask yourself the following: 'What is the key action?' Are there additional steps in the way of getting the key action (usually the purchase) to happen? For example, are you asking someone to create an account before they can buy? Why? You're creating an additional step—an obstacle—before they hand over their money. Are you making them fill in information you already have? Don't! Eliminate as many steps as you can, then time how long it takes to complete the buying process. If it's more than a few minutes, speed it up. Whatever you do, make the process easy.

Google suggests you focus on the following three steps to optimise for conversions[9]:

1. Eliminate steps
2. Anticipate needs
3. Make it fast and easy

Be aware of omni-channel jumping during the buying process. Forty per cent of consumers go from mobile to desktop to complete a purchase[10]. And 90 per cent of consumers say they use multiple devices, an average of three, to make decisions about a purchase. Make sure your journey is consistent across all platforms and devices.

Remember, humans are terrible at making choices. We need help to make the right choices. You have a huge opportunity to be there at the right time to help your customers make critical decisions. By

9 Google (2011) *Winning the Zero Moment of Truth.*
10 Google (2011) *Winning the Zero Moment of Truth.*

showing up to help consistently, by optimising for their experience, and by applying the good side of sales while burying the bad, you have a phenomenal opportunity to provide an exceptional decision experience for your customers. Do it right and they will come back for more. Do it intelligently with engagement tracking and you'll know when they're ready for more, before they do.

Sell: Real Life

Seeing is believing, so let's take a look at a company that's nailed the **Sell** phase through stellar segmentation and engagement-triggered sales. Keeping Current Matters is run by Bill and Charlotte Harney. The company was originally founded by Steve Harney, but Bill bought it from his dad and runs it with Charlotte.

Their mission in life is to help families make confident and educated decisions about housing. To do this, they offer a monthly membership that helps real estate agents understand the current housing market through content, educational resources, and so on, so they can help their clients make better decisions about buying or selling a home. They make the housing market, as complex as it is, simple to understand.

They are very clear on who they serve: their products are specifically for agents who see themselves as educators, not salespeople. To bring this mission to life, they start segmenting from the get-go: Keeping Current Matters attracts interest with daily blog content distributed via social media, and they use Infusionsoft by Keap by Keap opt-in forms to get lead information.

Because the content is good enough for existing members to frequently share it on social media (as it helps their clients too) they enjoy lovely native virality. KCM doesn't just post it up there and forget about it though; they promote blogs using paid advertising, using dozens of custom audiences to drive new and repeat traffic.

When agents land on the site, they're offered additional relevant content, e-guides, or webinars. The focus is always to ensure that no matter where someone comes from, or where they land, they're always being moved onto the next step in their journey, so more in-depth content is always on offer.

All new site visitors get added to a nurture campaign and lead-gen campaign on Facebook, retargeting visitors to bring them back to new content and build the relationship, before getting them to opt-in as a lead. Once a lead signs up, they immediately receive a welcome email series introducing the company, its purpose, and mission. Depending on what they've opted in for, leads then get a unique launch sequence lasting between three and five days. These sequences consist of additional content about the opt-in which then segues nicely into the next logical step, usually a free trial for the membership or a $7 entry offer. All of this is awesome, but things get really cool with what they call the 'merry-go-round'. Everyone gets a go on the merry-go-round!

The merry-go-round is a personalised nurture campaign that sends weekly emails to the entire database. That sounds quite standard, but it's much cooler than that—it tracks engagement and puts contacts into relevant sequences according to where their interests lie. The merry-go-round only ever offers content the prospect has already shown interest in. If a contact then engages with the content they're receiving, they automatically get added into relevant follow-up sequences. These follow-up sequences then make offers appropriate to what the consumer engages with and what they've seen previously.

The merry-go-round will then, of course, pull them out of the nurture to allow the contact to enjoy the targeted offer and follow-up. If the lead doesn't take the offer, they're added back into the nurture sequence until the next engagement.

This concept of offering according to engagement and segmentation has been a game changer. Previously, 57 per cent of Keeping Current Matters leads never received appropriate follow-up. The 43 per cent who were getting follow-up only ever got generic content that wasn't personalised based on their interests, engagement, or segmentation.

The merry-go-round and engagement tracking also allows Keeping Current Matters to mirror nurture content in retargeting campaigns on Facebook. So if the merry-go-round offers a lead an eBook, Facebook advertises them the same eBook. If they're offered a free trial, Facebook mirrors that offer. Prospects always receive the right message, at the right time, consistently across platforms and channels.

Keeping Current Matters' focus is on always providing the most useful and relevant content based on where the lead is in their customer journey right now, always getting them to the next step. With the merry-go-round cycling the best of their content, allowing for further segmentation, tracking engagement and then triggering relevant follow-up sequences and additional insights into new content, they're certain to offer the right thing to the consumer, because they are letting the consumer's behaviour inform them about their readiness to buy. This relentless focus allowed them to increase their membership by 36 per cent the first year, and 47 per cent the following year. They manage to convert 10 per cent of all leads to membership, and their super-targeted advertising and retargeting nets them a 373 per cent ROI for Facebook.

The $19.97 membership for real estate agents is their primary product, so all funnels lead to the very reasonably priced monthly subscription. They don't stop there, though.

A free trial offered on the site, in the merry-go-round, and on social media allows them to showcase the membership to their consumers. Consumers get a 'try before you buy' taste of what they'll get.

Every 14-day free-trial consumer also gets a Quick Start Programme. This six-sequence programme welcomes the trial member to the community, shows them round, and helps them navigate the members' area. It encourages members to use the membership, and helps them understand the vision and purpose of Keeping Current Matters.

The incredible nurture leads receive to help close the sale ensures they convert a ridiculous 80 per cent of free trials into paid memberships.

But what happens if the consumer doesn't complete the process of signing up for the trial itself? Here, KCM makes sure they don't lose a single lead. They discovered around 26 per cent of their leads were not completing the free trial sign-up.

To combat this conversion drop out, they instigated a catchment process and created a cart abandonment series to nurture leads that don't fully convert. These behaviour-driven processes mean KCM has managed to go from 50 members per month to over 500 since using Infusionsoft by Keap by Keap. That's a 1,000 per cent increase in members.

This personalised, content-heavy strategy has grown revenue from

$540,000 to almost $2,000,000—a 270 per cent increase. KCM's list has increased 400 per cent from 25,000 to 100,000. Looking at their traffic breakdown, it's clear how vital good qualifying content is to their success:

- 22 per cent of traffic comes from daily blog post subscriptions
- Three primary e-guides deliver 24 per cent of new leads
- Webinars produce 26 per cent of new leads, with a new webinar every six weeks on varying topics
- The free trial order form generates 27 per cent of leads, and even those who aren't ready to pay for membership get nurture

What Bill and Charlotte have done so well is provide the right information at the right time, in the right way. They've always focused on being relentlessly helpful, and they leverage that strategically to great effect, ensuring no lead is left without help in their decision-making process.

Sell: The Science & The Data

Purchase decisions are the climax of the efforts you've made to get consumers interested and ready to buy. At this crucial point, most businesses feel trepidation about the strategies they employ and often turn to the internet for validation.

As of the time of printing, searching for 'selling strategies' produces a whopping 170,000,000 results. I know when I started my own business I was incredibly wary of what other businesses suggested I do to sell my services. It was because of my own fear of being given terrible advice that I did so much research into the science behind selling. A sceptical mind is a strong mind.

Let me share what I've learned.

Now we've dug into the theory behind the **Sell** phase and looked at a case study, it's time to talk science. Here's the *why* behind what we've discussed so far.

As we touched on in previous chapters, in 2007 neuroscientist Professor Brian Knutson and his colleagues produced some ground-breaking research into how we buy[11]. They specifically wanted to look

11 Knutson, B., Rick, S., Wimmer, G.E., Prelec, D., & Loewenstein, G. (2007) 'Neural

at neural activity in the brain when we buy things. They were intrigued to see if this activity could help predict the likelihood of purchase. This phenomenal research gave us the purchase formula:

Net value = Reward − Pain.

To figure the formula out, they put subjects in an fMRI scanner and asked them to look at images of products. They then showed the price with the product and told participants to push a button if they'd buy it. When shown the product (a box of chocolates in one experiment) the brain displayed activity in the reward system. When we see something we want, our brain values the thing and says, 'Yes, I want this.'

The more the participants wanted something and the more value they perceived it had, the higher the activation in the reward centres. Conversely, of course, the lower the reward, the lower the activation. This seems logical and wasn't surprising. What *was* surprising was what happened next.

When participants were shown the price of a product, the area of the brain that deals with pain was activated: the insula. This area usually processes physical pain (like stubbing your toe) and social or emotional pain (like being bullied or excluded from social groups).

Because we evolved to survive, not to buy, our brain hacks itself to understand cost. Cost is the loss of something we have, and the closest thing we've evolved to deal with loss is pain. So the cost of the products is a loss of something we have—money—and we react by understanding that cost through pain. Price, therefore, equals pain. Similar to the reward activation, the higher the perceived cost, the more the insula was activated; the lower the perceived cost, the less the activation.

When participants wanted to purchase something, they always perceived the reward, then the cost. Their brains weighed up reward and cost, then chose whether or not to buy.

This relationship between pain and reward means the brain works out the net value of the purchase. It's an elegantly simple formula. By following the amount of reward activation versus the amount of pain activation, Knutson et al could predict the likelihood of purchase. They found the reward has to outweigh the pain. If it doesn't, the purchase won't happen.

This means we finally understand how to neurologically affect the purchase decision. We no longer have to rely on opinions on the internet—now we can use pure observable and fact-based science. Increase reward. Decrease cost.

The higher the net value of something, the more likely consumers are to purchase. Interestingly, because cost is always present, you can't omit pain entirely, which is why simply reducing prices doesn't mean consumers are more likely to buy. The biggest variable you can affect is to increase the perceived reward.

It's crucial to remember we're dealing with perceived value, not actual value. You don't need to actually increase the reward by adding more things to your offer, just increase the perceived value. You don't need to change your product; just change how your product is perceived. This perception is why some brands can charge more for the same item than other brands.

Perception also means there are implicit and explicit variables at play. Implicit variables are the things we can't put our fingers on. They are our gut feelings, and they indirectly affect how we perceive things.

Explicit variables are easily stated and direct. Consumers can tell you all the explicit reasons they choose certain products, yet they'll hardly ever touch on the role implicit variables play in choosing products. That is, in part, because System 1—the autopilot—controls the implicit variables.

The autopilot can't tell us explicitly why something is good or bad, that's not its function. It does, however, make us feel uneasy when something isn't quite right. For instance, in evolutionary terms, when all the birds in the jungle stopped singing we sensed something wasn't right, so there must be a predator near and we should be careful. We don't consciously think that, but we feel it and we're more cautious.

The 11 million bits a second of information the autopilot takes in are vital in giving us a good or bad feeling about something. In more modern times, when you're buying shampoo the autopilot takes in the shape and size of a bottle and determines whether it's fit for purpose, which this affects how we feel about it.

Or it looks at how the colours and font choice a brand uses makes us feel a certain way, and therefore more or less likely to buy. These implicit variables are vital to help us understand whether or not the purchase is for us, but they're completely subconscious. The autopilot processes them very quickly. It uses these implicit cues to understand where the product fits, so it can decide whether or not it's right before we pay effortful manual attention with the pilot (System 2). Together the two systems allow us to experience the world and make decisions.

In order for the two systems to work together, the autopilot uses frames of reference to understand context. Using learned experience, it looks at the context of a situation to decide whether it's a good fit.

Phil Barden gives a great example of this in his book *Decoded*—he studies the packaging of the Dynamic Pulse shower gel from Adidas[12]. It's a normal shower gel, so how does it stand out and get men to choose it over other shower gels in the supermarket?

First, look at the product itself: it's a refreshing and energising shower gel. It gives a nice oomph to your manly showering experience. But how does the company portray that, within a few seconds, to consumers looking at a shelf of products?

Here Adidas got clever. The bottle itself is shaped differently—it's similar to motor oil bottles. It's the same colour, too, and it has a section for good grip. The bottle is rugged, which means you can hold onto it firmly. The cap makes an intentional and satisfying click when you open it. Every implicit signal is of a high-performance, manly product.

The 11 million bits of information the autopilot takes in are all sorted into previous experience and all these individual signals are positive associations with high net value in the consumer's mind. That is, of course, if you *want* a manly, energising, high-performance shower!

Explicitly, the product's name is Dynamic Pulse.

The implicit and explicit align perfectly to create a specific frame of reference—a strong, manly shower experience.

However, if you wanted a luxurious shower you'd be looking for a different context—your motivation would be completely different and Dynamic Pulse wouldn't fit the frame, so you would ignore it. Dynamic Pulse has a high perceived value for the specific context of a manly,

12 Barden, P. (2013) *Decoded: The Science Behind Why We Buy*, John Wiley & Sons

energising shower. It fits all the implicit messages for the frame, and uses explicit language to back it up.

Framing is the precise reason some brands can demand more cash for the same product. The frame Aston Martin targets for cars is 'luxury' and 'prestige', and the price point they charge reflects that. The frame Toyota uses is 'economy' and 'family', and they price they charge reflects that.

The effect branding has on products has always been intangible, but we know now through various studies that brands affect the implicit context. Branding affects the frame and how the product is perceived. Nespresso is a perfect example of this[13].

In order to break into the coffee market, Nespresso had a problem. Their capsules are much pricier than the average granulated coffee you can buy in the shops. At 25 pence per capsule, they were massively overpriced compared to the rest of the market—or so customers thought. What they did to overcome this was genius. They changed the frame.

Rather than lumping themselves into the same frame as coffee you buy in supermarkets, Nespresso set their marketing up so they're compared with a proper espresso. Their marketing always involves a picture of the espresso itself and uses social context of celebrities to influence status. Using celebrities is run of the mill though; it's the espresso idea that's genius.

Espresso shots don't fit into the supermarket granulated coffee frame. They're not even in the context of ground coffee or beans. The context of espresso is coffee shops. The average price of a coffee in a shop with baristas is around £3 to £5. In comparison, 25 pence is a minor expenditure.

Nespresso owned the frame of having barista coffee at home, using special capsules. This increased the perceived value and the customer's willingness to pay a premium price. Nespresso carefully controlled their frame with implicit variables and hugely increased its perceived value. Find your ideal frame, and own it with implicit variables.

But what about explicit variables? To explicitly increase the perceived value of your product, you can use value adding language

13 Barden, P. (2013) *Decoded: The Science Behind Why We Buy*, John Wiley & Sons

because language affects context and has a physical impact on neuronal processing in the value centres of the brain.

A fascinating study by de Araujo et al on the perception of odour and labels showed us how we label a certain smell can actually affect whether or not we perceive it as pleasant, even if it's the same smell[14].

In the test, cheese odour was labelled 'cheddar cheese' or 'body odour'. Despite the odour being exactly the same, the label affected whether or not participants enjoyed the smell. This effect was visible in the reward centres of the brain in an fMRI scanner. Flowery language actually makes products more appealing physically.

There are many ways to increase perceived value, but let's look at decreasing perceived cost. Remember, we're talking about affecting the *perceived* cost, not the actual cost.

Hilke Plassmann performed another fMRI experiment looking at how cost affects perception and enjoyment[15]. He gave participants various types of wine and told them the price. The more expensive wines benefited from increased enjoyment. Wine quality is extremely variable, which is why the cost varies—or so wine manufacturers would have you think.

Plassmann also gave participants the same wine twice, telling them it was expensive the first time, and cheap the next time. Despite the wine being exactly the same, participants enjoyed the more expensive version far more, and reward activation increased with the price.

These participants were being implicitly manipulated by price. The autopilot has learned by association that more money often means better wine, so the frame for the more expensive wine set them up to enjoy it more. The higher cost actually increased the perceived value, so it's important not to drop the price of your products to try to increase the value.

This is why old-school marketers often tell you to add a zero to

---

14 de Araujo, I. E., Rolls, E. T., Velazco, M. I., Margot, C., & Cayeux, I. (2005) 'Cognitive modulation of olfactory processing', Neuron, 46(4), 671–79.

15 Plassmann, H. et al. (2007) 'Orbitofrontal Cortex Encodes Willingness to Pay in Everyday Economic Transactions', *Journal of Neuroscience*, 27 (37), 9984–88; and Plassmann, H., O'Doherty, J., Shiv, B., & Rangel, A. (2008) 'Marketing actions can modulate neural representations of experienced pleasantness', *Proceedings of the National Academy of Sciences* (USA), 105(3), 1050–54

the end of your product prices. Don't do it rashly or without thought, though; it can be terrible advice because the frame needs to be appropriate, too.

If you want to charge a premium price, all your implicit signals must be of a premium service. If the frame doesn't fit the price, the formula won't work and consumers won't commit because it 'feels' wrong. This is why Nespresso had to carefully control its frame to ensure it could justify the premium pricing.

So there are implicit and explicit impacts, and costs, too. Crucially, instead of altering the price, we can control the perception of cost. Choose your frame wisely and use pricing to match it.

There are other ways to decrease the perceived cost, too. Phil Barden breaks down how Steve Jobs used anchoring to carefully control the frame when he released the iPad[16]. Rather than have it compared to other products, he discussed how the product is worth $999.

During the presentation, his slide displayed $999 in large type on the screen. Then he clicked to the next slide and $999 was crushed by a falling $499. He completely removed the possibility of his audience comparing the iPad to the then very common and much cheaper notebook by anchoring people on $999 then switching the real price out. People compared the iPad to its own price.

In *Priceless: The Myth of Fair Value*, William Poundstone describes a similar effect from an MIT study run in catalogues[17]. By showing the sale price next to the pre-sale price, consumers could understand the price difference, they anchored on the pre-sale price and could see exactly how much of a deal they were getting. Anchoring enabled consumers to clearly experience the perception of the decrease in price.

Money is not the only cost, though; there are also time and behaviour costs associated with purchasing. Consumers will pay more money for a product they perceive as saving them time. Once we start a process we're happier to wait than if we haven't yet started. Consumers want to feel momentum; if you can give that to them they'll pay well for it.

And then, of course, there is behaviour. Behavioural costs are why

---

16 Barden, P. (2013) *Decoded: The Science Behind Why We Buy*, John Wiley & Sons
17 Poundstone, P. (2011) *Priceless: The Myth of Fair Value (and How to Take Advantage of It)*. Hill & Wang

having an easy and streamlined process is so important. The most famous example of conversion-rate optimisation due to behavioural cost is from Luke Wroblewski[18]. In the case study, he mentions how a simple button tweak to make the buying process easier earned the company an additional $300 million.

Essentially the purchase process initially included creating an account so returning visitors could easily buy again. Instead, it added an obstacle in the way of people purchasing. By removing the account creation step and adding a simple 'you do not need to create an account to purchase' message, the company went on to increase sales by 45 per cent. Make it easy for people to spend their money with you, and you decrease the perceived cost to their time and effort expended.

With all the above in mind, let's take a look at why it's important to contrast and differentiate your offer.

Value and cost are extremely relative. In *Predictably Irrational* (a goldmine for businesses looking to get ahead) Dan Ariely discusses the pricing choices for *The Economist*[19]. Originally their pricing structure was as follows:

- Web only: $59
- Print only: $ 125
- Print and Web: $125

$59 seems like a reasonable price to pay for something, but the contrast between print-only and print-and-web is easy to understand. If you choose print-and-web, you get two things for the same price as getting print-only. It's a no-brainer.

And that is exactly what consumers did. Only 16 per cent chose web only. Eighty-four per cent opted for print-and-web, a full zero per cent for print-only.

Because no one ever chose print only, *The Economist* removed the option altogether. Suddenly, the web-only option became the most popular and was chosen 68 per cent of the time. The print-and-web option fell to *least* popular, chosen only 32 per cent of the time.

18 Spool, J.M. (2009) *The $300 Million Button* https://articles.uie.com/three_hund_million_button/
19 Ariely, D. (2009) *Predictably Irrational: The Hidden Forces That Shape Our Decisions.* Harper

It turns out, the print-only option was not useless at all, it provided a contrast. It decreased the perceived cost of the print-and-web option and gave *The Economist* a boost of 43 per cent in value of sales. This effect is often referred to as 'coherent arbitrariness'[20]—the effect of setting an arbitrary baseline and watching the effect on behaviour.

Scientifically, neurons only respond to differences and changes. As we can't assign value to something in a vacuum, we must have comparison between two options.

To summarise, in order to use the advances neuroscience has given us, your intentional actions must be to relentlessly increase the net value of your products or services. Focus on increasing the rewards and decreasing the cost using both implicit and explicit variables, and controlling the frames consumers use to compare and contrast your products.

Then make it easy to buy—don't get in the way of consumers who want to give you their money.

20 Ariely, D., Loewenstein, G. & Prelec, D. (2003) '"Coherent Arbitrariness": Stable Demand Curves Without Stable Preferences', *The Quarterly Journal of Economics*, 118(1), 73–106

The Brain Hack

Humans evolved to survive, not to buy—so the brain doesn't understand the concept of cost during the buying process. To get around this, the brain hacked itself by understanding cost as pain.

When we buy something, we part with hard-earned resources—money—and parting with resources isn't good for survival. Buying stuff is *literally* painful to us.

So if you want your customers to decide to purchase something from you, you must...

Hack Your Buyer's Brain

To hack your buyer's brain, focus relentlessly on increasing the perceived reward and decreasing the perceived cost of your offering. Use implicit and explicit variables to help brains create frames to understand value and to differentiate.

Use BANT content to help you leadscore and segment your audience into customer profiles for better engagement.

And, of course, make it easy to buy: the cost to your customer isn't just in money; if it's awkward to hand over cash, it costs us time and effort—which is also painful.

CHAPTER 6: Wow—Knock Their Socks Off

*"Do what you did in the beginning of a rela-
tionship and there won't be an end."*

~ Anthony Robbins

CHAPTER 6: Wow—Knock Their Socks Off

Wow: The Principle & The Problem

Yes! You got the purchase—job done! Congratulations and drinks all round! Except the round is on you, and you don't have any cash because that customer you just converted has gone and left you for another provider...

Oh dear!

Even if you only sell products people can buy in isolation, if you let your customers walk at this point you let your profits walk with them. It's easy to assume that once you've got the purchase you can pack up and go home. The reality, however, is that when you've made the sale you still have work to do. It's now your job to provide an exemplary experience for that new customer. It's time for fulfilment.

But does that mean you should palm off your new customer to the fulfilment team and run back to the beginning of the whole buying process? Absolutely not. Remember your consumer doesn't gives a rat's bottom about your silos and departments. All they care about is whether or not you deliver what you promise, and that you do it well.

153

After purchase, consumers go through their Second Moment of Truth: the experience. Looking back to moments of truth, the Zero Moment of Truth was finding out what they wanted and needed, then clarifying it.

The First Moment of Truth was when they found precisely what they wanted and decided to buy it.

Now the Second Moment of Truth is the point at which they actually have the product and start using it. This is where they decide if your product is any good or not, and if it's fulfilling expectations and delivering what they need. The customer experiences what they've just bought. And this vital moment is when they decide whether or not your service or product is any good. If you run away and start selling to someone else at this point, you'll only prove to them that they weren't important to you and all you care about is the next sale. The Second Moment of Truth is really an extension of your sales process—and a vital one, at that. Because if you get this wrong you'll lose out on ever doing business with that customer again.

Your focus at this point should be on extending customer lifetime value. Customer lifetime value is arguably the most important number every business should strive to improve. While there are few different formulae for different types of business, it generally boils down to:

The amount of time you retain a customer X (How much they spend with you in a period of time – The cost of getting them / keeping them)

Work out what your current baseline average customer lifetime value (CLV) is now. Go ahead, I'll wait here.

Once you know what your average CLV is, you can work on increasing it. Bain and Company found businesses that focus on customer lifetime value and retain just an additional 5 per cent of customers can increase their profits by between 25 and 95 per cent[1]. That is *huge*.

The same study showed that because those consumers have an existing relationship with you, it costs 600 to 700 per cent less to retain them than get a new customer on board. Those same customers will continue to bring in more money, too.

1 Reichheld, F. (2001) 'Prescription for Cutting Costs', Bain & Company www.bain.com/insights/prescription-for-cutting-costs-bain-brief/

Bain and Company also identified that repeat customers spend more and generate larger transactions the longer they stick around (67 per cent larger purchases in months 31–36 than in months 0–6). Even better, they refer more people to you. Their study showed that a happy one-time purchaser will refer three people—but after ten purchases they refer seven people. So that's more profits, more frequent, larger purchases, and more new customers.

Customer lifetime value isn't just for fun, there's serious money in it. It's a win-win for you and for the consumer—they're happy, and you get repeat purchases and more customers. Who knew it would pay so handsomely to be nice to your consumers? Funny that.

In the long run, your customers decide your revenue. You can leave it up to them, or you can do everything you can to ensure they're happy and bringing you good customer lifetime value. All you need to do is focus on giving them the best experience possible. So as it turns out, purchase one is like winning a battle—but you still need to win the war. And, like most wars, it's highly profitable for the winners and painful for the losers.

Being the loser here is far easier than you'd think. Being a winner means you're looking after your consumers, and they're spending money and feeling happy about it. Being the loser doesn't mean you're the opposite of that—losing customers and not getting repeat purchases from those who do stay—it also means apathy.

Apathy is a killer because customers don't feel anger or resentment, which are both easy to spot. It's simply a lack of enthusiasm or concern. Sixty-eight per cent of customers leave a brand because of indifference[2]. Your customers leave simply because they can't be bothered to stay. That means anything more exciting than nothing that comes along has the potential to entice them away—which is worryingly easy.

In part, this is because straight after purchase businesses drop their new customers and run all the way back to the front of the customer journey again to grab another new customer. This seems like a logical thing to do, but in reality it's a waste of time and effort. Focus on ensuring apathy does not set in. Don't lose the consumer because they

2 John Gattorna (2008) www.customerthermometer.com/customer-satisfaction/csat-stat-68-percent/

feel like they've been used and you don't love them anymore. Instead, retain just 5 per cent more of your existing consumers and make them happy—they'll spend more cash to up your profits. In theory, this shouldn't be too hard. In practice, however, it's tough to remember to focus on your new customers—most businesses just leave the newbies to get on with it.

Inside The Buyer Brain

The initial moment after purchase is an emotional high for your customer. The brain is flooded with dopamine and the consumer is happy because they anticipate a reward. If you're not careful, though, it's all downhill from there. The excitement slowly wears off and the customer hits a lull similar to when they first tentatively started the buying process (see Figure 4). Instead of letting that happen, focus on small interactions to increase the excitement level. You want the graph to even out to a straightish line (as in Figure 5) rather than a drop. If you let the magic fade, buyer's remorse will take over.

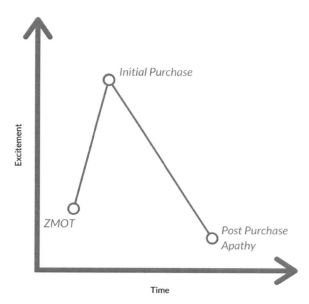

Figure 4: Customer excitement levels in the sales process

It's generally in the post-purchase lull that most businesses reach out and offer more products and services—but the problem is the consumer is now at their lowest ebb. That's even worse than selling to them cold, because now they feel apathetic about you. Instead, keep the excitement and happiness topped up.

After purchase, something interesting happens that you can take advantage of: the post-purchase consumption point. In the Second Moment of Truth, consumers experience a mini research point. They look for best practices and tips, community and support, implementation guides and ideas. This is especially prevalent in the B2B community, where buying cycles are protracted and easy to spot. Consumers look for more content. They want validation. They want support. They want more information. They are actively crying out for engagement and you have the power to give it to them.

You have an opportunity here to nurture your new customers with valuable information about their purchase. Nurture isn't just for the initial engagement—post-purchase nurture can help you win a

Figure 5: Maintaining customer excitement levels post-purchase

customer for life. Take advantage of this desire for more information and make sure you welcome your new consumers on board warmly. Think of your welcome as your first handshake with a new customer. Tell them who you are as a business, tell them why you care, and at the same time pre-empt the questions they're looking for answers to.

Provide them with best practices, as well as information to help them use your product or service successfully. Develop your relationship and humanise the buying process where possible. Make your customer feel special, because if you don't, your competition will.

Ask yourself how your introductory process makes your customer feel. Are they proud to say they just bought from you, or is it more of an awkward walk of shame?

What about your second conversation—how does that make them feel? Remember you need to personalise for nurture, not the **Sell**. You have the sale already—now work on developing the relationship.

Marketo states that 80 per cent of consumers (global) only engage with a brand's marketing offers if they're based on how they previously interacted with the brand[3]. You have the information you need now, so use it.

Google tells us people are more loyal to their need in the moment than to any brand, and that 65 per cent of people look for the most relevant information when searching, regardless of who's providing that information[4].

So after purchase, and after welcoming them, focus on providing your customers with the information they're looking for. To build a long customer relationship, make using your products habitual, or make turning to you in their moment of need habitual. You can't do either of these things if you're not keeping in touch and keeping the emotional journey topped up.

That means doing all the work you did to get your consumer to buy in the first place *after* they've bought from you, as well. Give them quality content. That doesn't mean you need to go off and create new content—very often you can use existing content you've created to get people in the door in the first place. The crucial thing is to send people

---

3 Marketo, *The 5 Principles of Engagement Marketing.*
4 Google (2011) *Winning the Zero Moment of Truth.*

information, add value, and track engagement so you know when they're ready for the next step in their journey.

Let's take a look at how you get solid customer lifetime value. How do you ensure consumers turn to you habitually, enjoy it, buy more of your products or services, stay loyal in the moment, and rave about you to their family and friends?

Wow: The Solution

When consumers purchase, their first action is to consume what they've bought. Inventively, this is most often referred to as the consumption journey. Here, your job is to first get them to use their purchase, then to satisfy their research points, and finally to make sure they're happy. To achieve this you need a killer post-purchase nurture strategy, with check-ins and solid nurture points. Luckily, behavioural economics and lifecycle marketing have your back.

First, let's take a look at each component of the consumption journey:

↓ Research

↓ Implementation (usage)

↓ Proving

↓ Optimisation (owning)

↓ Enjoying

Straight after purchase, consumers look at what they've purchased— this is the Second Moment of Truth—then they do a little research on what other people are doing with their product and discover how they can best use it. This point of learning can be a quick and simple process (a simple internal reflection) looking at how other people are using the product, or perhaps reading the user guide, or it can be a much longer and more protracted process, depending on the complexity of the product or service.

Next, the customer will try it out or play around with it. At that point they'll start to reflect internally about whether or not the product does what it said it would, whether it was worth the price, and if it suits or fits their criteria. This is where consumers build their own opinions— and they borrow bits of other opinions from their initial research. If the product or service fits the initial criteria, they'll tweak and refine their opinions, start to optimise their use of the product, and alter their opinion towards it and own it.

And finally, if this is a positive process, the customer moves into the **Enjoying** phase. Next time they have to perform this process, it'll be much faster because they now have their own baseline to use. This journey holds true for buying coffee at Starbucks or taking up a new hobby or using new software at work.

For example, let's imagine buying a coffee for the first time. The process goes something like this:

1. **Purchase:** Choose options, buy coffee, tell barista my name, barista tells me to stand at the end counter and wait for my name to be called.

2. **Research:** I am in the right place—waiting at the end like I've been told. There are other people here—I feel validated that I'm in the right place. I can smell coffee being ground and prepared, I can see and hear it being made.

3. **Internal reflection and validation:** What is everyone else in the line buying and collecting? Did I get the right coffee? What else could I have bought?

4. **Decision:** I'm satisfied with what I got, but I might try a caramel latte next time.

5. **Implementation (usage):** I pick up the cup when my name is called. Barista confirmed who I am and what I ordered—I have the right order.

6. **Proving:** It is hot—it should be. Small sip, is it the right coffee? Yes, it was made appropriately. It tastes like it should, and it is what I ordered. It fulfils my criteria.

7. **Optimisation/Owning:** I need to add sugar and stir it.

8. **Enjoying:** Good, it's just how I like it. I am satisfied.

For a relatively small purchase like this, the process goes quickly and without much conscious thought, but your autopilot would constantly process your experience, adding to how you feel about it so next time you can order with far less effort.

While this may seem a silly example, I specifically chose it not only to show you that this process is universal, but also because Starbucks has worked relentlessly on the experience their consumers go through after purchasing their coffee.

They broke up the process of ordering into two parts, so consumers were more comfortable waiting for the coffee—this makes them part of the process and happier to wait. The barista asks for a name so customers own their cup when it's called, and they repeat the order so you know it's yours. You can see, hear, and smell the coffee being made so you know what's happening at each stage. You can see what other people are buying so you feel like you're part of a group of people who do that sort of thing.

The entire journey is planned and mapped out so you own the process and are more likely to come back again next time. In more complex journeys, the process you go through is far more obvious, but it takes the same steps. Let's take a look at a process with a higher learning curve, buying a new camera:

1. **Purchase:** Choose criteria, buy camera, wait for it to be delivered.

2. **Research:** I can track the delivery and I know when it will arrive.

3. **Internal reflection and validation:** What will I need to learn in order to use it? Find the user guide on the internet and start reading; it looks complicated. Did I get the right camera? Will I be able to use it effectively? Look for information on how to do things with camera. What else could I have bought? What cameras are other people using to take pictures? Yes, those are the types of people I would associate with and their pictures look good.

4. **Decision:** I'm satisfied with what I got and I feel validated.

5. **Implementation (usage):** Unpacking the camera, I'm excited it has arrived. Move to switch it on, the battery isn't charged—I'm frustrated because now I have it I want to use it. Plug it in and charge it. Read the user guide. When it's charged, switch it on and start learning to use it.

6. **Proving:** Take a lot of pictures, initially of boring things. Does it work? Yes, it does. It takes pictures, and it is what I ordered. It fulfils my criteria. But now I need to learn how to use it properly.

7. **Optimisation/Owning:** I need to learn how to use the camera properly, and I need to learn how to take good photographs. I need to practise and using the camera needs to become habitual.

8. **Enjoying:** I can take OK pictures, people are impressed with my new camera, I enjoy going out and taking pictures of cows. I am satisfied.

The process of buying and using the camera is much more protracted, and there are much larger obstacles to overcome. This is because camera companies haven't made it easy to learn how to use their cameras properly. They haven't optimised the experience in the same way Starbucks has.

The key is to make the experience smooth and pleasant, removing as many obstacles as possible.

Let's take a look at how you can plan this process for yourself now. The final stage in lifecycle marketing is called **Wow**, and this phase is all about the consumption journey. **Wow** is about making sure your consumer has the best experience possible, that they're happy, and that they refer people to you, give you testimonials, buy more, and are even more delighted.

The **Wow** stage is built precisely to help you get customer lifetime value, which is pretty awesome. It consists of:

- Deliver and Wow
- Offer more
- Testimonials and referrals

Let's take a deep dive into each of the stages within this phase.

Deliver & Wow

Deliver and Wow is where you do what you said you would do and deliver whatever it is the consumer has purchased. It's crucial to go above and beyond and give your customer an experience that wows them.

Delivering the product is the least you need to do here. There's no **Wow** in doing what you said you'd do—that's just keeping up your end of the bargain. Simply providing your customer with what they've purchased doesn't win you any medals. If you want a happy customer, **Wow** them.

At this point in their consumption journey your customer actively looks for information and compares what they've purchased with what others have bought, just like standing in line in Starbucks judging what everyone else is buying. This is the Second Moment of Truth and a research point.

To provide value here, you must provide valuable information and help your customer to start using their product. It's also your opportunity to welcome them on board. Don't let your first handshake be limp-wristed. Thank them for becoming a customer, welcome them warmly, and tell them who you are and why you care—and also provide the valuable information they're looking for and that will help them get the most out of their new product or service.

The information you provide is called post-purchase nurture. As you've nurtured consumers to the point of sale, so the very nature of this post-purchase nurture is to continue to build the relationship. Focus on helping your consumer and making their implementation as streamlined as possible.

Whether it's simply clear instructions on what to do next (as Starbucks aims to achieve during their process) or more complex details on how to get the best out of your product, help your consumer implement their use of their new product. People like to research some specific topics people during this stage—use them yourself to get a head start:

- Best practices
- Community (people love to see how people like them are going through a similar process)
- Implementation guides
- Inspiration
- How-to

During this post-purchase nurture, the consumer is totally focused on making the product work. They want to ensure a smooth process, check the product or service meets expectations, and know their needs are met. Your job is simply to make sure they experience that smooth process. Pro tip: some purchases come with instant delivery— but if there's a delay, or if it will take a day or a few weeks, it's vital to communicate this to your customer and keep updating them as to when they can expect to receive their new product. This prevents people from getting frustrated and keeps them excited about their purchase.

But your job is far from done just yet—from here, your customer moves to proving then owning. The more a new customer uses your product, the more they'll like it; this odd little bias is called the 'mere exposure' effect, so exploit it to put some habits in place and get people primed to like your stuff.

After the initial excitement dies down, customers move into the proving phase. By now they should have received their product and be actively using it. Here the consumer wants to assess success. Did they achieve the benefits you promised? What's their momentum like—are they stuck, or moving along with their product nicely? Can they see a ROI—or will they see their return soon?

ROI can be monetary, emotional, or time-based and your product should help them achieve at least one of those. You can make money when you buy something, either by saving money or making money through using the product or service. You can save yourself hassle and heartache, you can experience increased happiness or decreased stress. And you can save time. Show your eager consumer how your product or service has done one of these things for other people.

It's important to note they may not have completely achieved these benefits yet, but they should at least see progress. If the ROI is more protracted, help them understand that it's coming. Inspire them. The customer's ideal outcome is to be satisfied with the solution and see positive ROI, which is one step closer to a satisfied customer.

From here we move into optimisation. This is another research point for consumers, and it's where they actively compare how they're doing to how other people are doing. This is also the ownership stage. At this point, a happy customer believes the solution is great, and they're happy with the company who provided it. They want to see proof and evidence that it made their life easier or better in some way. Their ideal outcome is get a good ROI—whether it be money, time, or emotion.

Your customer should value your product: you want them to be happy, and you want them to feel like you looked after them at every stage of their buying journey.

Now you have them as a customer and kept the excitement high at every opportunity, ask how they're getting on. It's time to contact them and find out if they're happy. If they *are* happy, awesome—we can move on to the second stage of the **Wow** phase. But if they aren't happy, you have a perfect opportunity to fix it if you can. Another pro tip—you can track customer behaviour throughout the buying process by looking at how they're engaging with you, so you can pre-empt any problems.

Offer More

Providing your customer is happy, you now have the opportunity to move them onto their next step and increase value. The value goes both ways: for you as a business, by increasing their customer lifetime value; and for them, by improving their lives even more.

There are different ways to do this, but first make sure the customer is happy. There are few things more damaging than offering a new product to an unhappy consumer—if they were starting to feel like you didn't care about them, you'll justify that feeling and they'll feel like you're just milking them for their money. So be sure to find out how they're doing, or at the very least check their engagement levels to ensure they'll be receptive to your message. Once you're sure, you can deploy some tactics to offer more products, where appropriate.

Offering more to consumers is often referred to as up-selling. The use of 'up-sell' here is actually a bastardisation of the term, so let's set the record straight.

What we often innocently, but sometimes lazily, refer to as up-selling is actually four different things:

- Up-selling
- Cross-selling

- Down-selling
- New products

Up-selling is the act of getting consumers to level-up their purchase—which is directly related to their current purchase. If you have something to help them achieve their desired end result quicker, that's an up-sell. This may be special treatment or a premium service.

If you're simply offering them anything to raise their order amount, it's not an up-sell, it's a cross-sell. A cross-sell is often an ideal product or service-pairing that will enhance their experience. It's not always directly related to the product purchased, it's a cool add-on. For example, adding car hire to your flight purchase is a cross-sell.

You can offer a down-sell when a consumer has said no to something—but you may have a cheaper alternative they can choose. If you've run out of what they originally wanted, you can offer a down-sell as another option. For instance, if standing tickets to your favourite band have sold out, you might be offered seated tickets at the back of the venue. It's not what you originally wanted, but it's better than not going (and often cheaper).

Finally, new products are things you should notify your consumers about when they come out. They may not be aware of your new products and will likely purchase them if it fits with their desired outcomes.

The perfect time to offer these additional options is at the point of optimisation. If the customer wants to level-up their product use, they may be happy to make extra purchases to achieve this. They may not be aware of perfect product pairings, and may be more than just willing to enhance their lives with some of your other products—they may be eager for it. If your customer looks for how to get the best out of what they have, they're pushing it further. Be there with appropriate offers to help them make their desired outcome happen.

But how do you know if they're ready for another offer?

Well, if you're already engaging them with post-purchase nurture, you can leadscore customer engagement. As I mentioned previously, leadscoring is tracking their behaviour, creating your own formula for what makes a good prospect, and assigning points for positive engagements while subtracting them for negative behaviour.

Leadscoring is generally reserved for the initial sales process, but it shouldn't be. You can continuously identify which customers will be ready to buy more if you leadscore them continually. This enables you to put together some solid segmentation based on their interests so, when it comes to offering more, you have all the information you need.

Find out which of your products or services are often purchased together, or find items consumers consider to be 'must-haves' based on previous buying history, and you'll be able to identify what the next logical product is in their customer journey. These are 'product associations'. Associate your products together to discover what the next logical step is for your customer.

If you don't know what the next logical step is, or there isn't an obvious step, you can use a sneaky little trick to find out what they're interested in. I call this a segmentation cascade (no sexy names here I'm afraid).

The basic premise is to choose three products your customer could buy next then create nurture content related to each of those three products. For instance, if a consumer booked flights with an airline, and the airline wanted to offer them more but isn't sure what the customer needs, and had hotel offers, car offers, and package offers, the airline could create good content about each of those three things then drip that content out to customers and track what they engaged with. If they engaged with the car-related nurture content, not hotel or package content, you could offer them car deals.

This is a great way to figure out what someone may be interested in. It's called a cascade because if they aren't interested in one topic, you cascade them onto the next content. It's an effective strategy because you use nurture content to track interest, so they won't get cross with you for selling at them all the time.

Another way to get your consumers to buy more is to offer incentives for repeat purchasing. These are loyalty schemes and can work amazingly well to get your consumers habitually using your service or products instead of the competition's.

To start putting a loyalty programme together properly, or to critique your existing programme, find out if your consumer is loyal in certain areas, or if they're simply loyal overall. You may find your consumers are loyal to you for one specific thing, but not others.

What happens if they step out of your bubble in search of more information for specific products? What will they find? If you focus on when you want to own loyalty, you can be fantastically targeted with your loyalty incentives. Saying you want loyalty isn't enough. When do you want it? And how is it performing for you now?

Referrals & Testimonials

If you provide a stellar experience for your customers—if you look after them and check in on them often, and you offer more where appropriate—your customers should be successfully wowed! Congratulations!

You're well on your way to achieving strong customer lifetime value. Once consumers are wowed, they pass into the **Enjoying** phase of the consumption journey. Here, customers should be using their product or service comfortably and having a good time doing it. Their new product should be improving their quality of life, and they will probably have taken you up on some additional offers. If they continue to enjoy the experience you've designed for them, they'll become loyal, then hopefully an advocate.

We want every consumer to be an advocate (or evangelist). These are the people who tell their friends and family about you whenever they get the chance. They talk about you on social media and they are all-round completely besotted with you. That's the holy grail!

Finding who your advocates are is of paramount importance because these people are willing to help you provide invaluable social proof to new leads in the form of testimonials and referrals. You can measure their engagement levels and ask how they're getting on using surveys, net promoter scores, calls, and simply reaching out.

However you contact your advocates, the social proof they give you provides phenomenal sway for new leads to purchase other products, so do everything you can to capture them. Your happy customers will be willing to help you, but make it easy for them to do so and effective for you by structuring your testimonial requests. Here are seven questions you can ask:

- What problem led you to look for a product like this in the first place?

- What was the obstacle that would have prevented you from buying this product?
- What did you find as a result of buying this product?
- What specific feature did you like most about this product?
- What are three other benefits of this product?
- Would you recommend this product? If so, why?
- Is there anything you'd like to add?

Structuring the testimonial this way enables you to pull specific and useful information out of your customers that your leads and prospects will identify with. It gives you a story to tell.

This type of testimonial is far more effective because it actually speaks to the concerns and problems other prospects have.

Make sure that if your lovely customers do give you a testimonial, you reward them with a personalised thank you to deepen your relationship. Whatever you do, though, don't bribe them beforehand. You may get more testimonials that way, but it's unethical and underhanded, and consumers can tell which testimonials have been coerced. We're primed to uncover a lack of authenticity, and it's not wise to gamble with trust.

But what about referrals, which is when your customer tells other people to use your services or products? Getting quality referrals can be tricky. If you incentivise this, you may get poor-quality referrals because the referrer only makes the recommendation so they get the incentive. And remember, customers won't often suggest their family or friends get in touch if they think you're going to hit their contact with the hard-sell.

So how can you capitalise on your good relationship and get better referrals? One option is to make sure you offer such an amazing experience people want to shout about you (you should definitely do that!). But the other option is to help people be better friends to their buddies. To get ahead in the referral game, tap into our innate desire to be better people to our in-group (our friends and family). In order to be a better person in the in-group, we need to make people's lives better—and you can enable your consumer to do that. If you have invaluable resources, special gifts, and unique offers for your consumers to bestow upon their friends, you can help them be a better friend. Give them something of high value to their in-group and unique to your advocates.

Make sure your customers have an amazing experience and nurture them through their consumption journey, then check in with them and offer more where appropriate. Reward loyalty and learn from your advocates. If you do all this, you will deliver an awesome **Wow** experience. You'll touch all the salient points on the consumption journey and you'll improve your customer lifetime journey.

But don't stop there. Keep the relationship alive by continually keeping in touch with valuable content and information. One of the easiest ways to do this is by using existing content and any new content you create as a form of long-term nurture.

Track their engagement and use that information to inform you when consumers are ready to be offered more (we'll discuss the long-term nurture more in Chapter 7). Always focus on building a valuable relationship with your consumer and rewarding them for that relationship.

Let's take a look at how one business did all of the above and more, and grew—despite its head honcho ending up out of action for nearly a year.

Wow: Real Life

The Brooklyn Music Factory (BMF) is a music school in Brooklyn, New York, and it's an awesome example of **Wow** done right. After spending 20+ years teaching private music lessons and watching kids get a great start but not following through with their talents, eventually leading to kids giving up music, Nate Shaw was determined to develop the missing link between what makes music enjoyable and what makes kids stick with it.

When you start learning to make music, you learn alone. But by focusing on developing a community, Nate was determined to get children comfortable jamming together, building musical fluency, and having fun. And so BMF was born with this mission:

'Through game-based learning, we give students the tools needed to make music with other musicians.'

From the age of four, children can learn to make music together from the very beginning. At the age of 14, children become MITs—Musicians In Training. MITs help with band classes, studio maintenance, fixing things, and with setting up the live gigs, etc. This creates the community vibe and teaches the kids transferable skills.

But it's not only the kids who get to join in: the BMF approach to music includes the whole family. They offer adult bands and lessons, and their ideal customer is a family with 75 per cent or more of its members making music together. To achieve this aim, they provide lessons, workshops, seminars, panel discussions, expert sessions and the like to help people see there's so much more to the music industry than just performing.

After reading *The E-Myth*[5], Nate decided automation wasn't going to detract from and depersonalise his business, so he invested in Infusionsoft by Keap by Keap to automate his sales and marketing. He wanted to personalise the experience as much as possible, so when he started automating he moved away from just trying to generate leads and moved towards better nurturing his existing community of music lovers. This allowed BMF to make each family's experience better. Purely because of that, families started to increase their investment, which in turn made students perform better.

Nate finally started tracking the monthly family spend (their version of customer lifetime value) and has focused on increasing it year on year. Initially, BMF used traditional marketing like flyers and batch and blast emails, to convert leads—but when BMF moved to Infusionsoft by Keap by Keap it dumped its list and only kept the 130 families they were working with at the time.

It was a risky move, but Nate was determined to focus more on the families and community aspect of the business. With that relentless focus, his list has grown from 130 families to 1,900 families within two years—purely by word-of-mouth referrals.

---

5 Gerber, M.E. (2001) *The E-Myth Revisited: Why Most Small Businesses Don't Work and What to Do About It* (2nd rev ed)., HarperBusiness

Nate realised he can't just rely on families coming to lessons, so he sends families great content like blogs, YouTube videos, and more—and focuses on answering questions the community asked via highly targeted emails. This way the community requests the content he's providing, so it's always of high value because it's answering the questions they have asked.

BMF also uses engagement with RSVPs to events, seminars, and concerts to segment families' unique interests. Mass marketing is a no-no, and this finely tuned segmentation means they can have more personalised conversations with their audience.

BMF shows families how to guide their child from being a happy beginner to a highly committed life-long musician, not just through lessons but through content too—and the engagement speaks for itself.

BMF's nurture process is slow and organic because they understand it's not about a semester of lessons here and there. The average customer lifetime for a child at BMF is between 10 and 14 *years*. Because Nate knows this, he can focus on getting leads in the right way, knowing his retention is super-high and that families will stick around.

To get families in the door, BMF offers entry-level classes for a low financial investment. They make sure the families get the **Wow** experience within their first year, so they become an active, committed part of the community and events.

With a relentless focus on community, the experience, and the lifetime value of his families, Nate grew the Brooklyn Music Factory from just 63 families in 2010 to 263 families in 2015, a steady 25–30 per cent growth year-on-year, with each family sticking around for ten or more years, spending more every year.

That's astounding customer lifetime value in action.

Nate's passion is one of my favourite studies into how **Wow** can be so powerful, because he exemplifies the process. He knew that by relentlessly focusing on the experience his consumers would become advocates and refer his ideal clients to him in a way that advertising could not match.

Amazingly, despite needing open-heart surgery and not being able to work at all during his months of medical leave, his business still grew by 5 per cent. This is in part due to the automation he set up in advance—but I believe it's mostly because BMF focuses on keeping consumers happy and genuinely improving their lives. His philosophy helps him drive continual growth.

I tip my hat to Nate. He is an amazing example of impassioned crafting of the customer experience, and he's reaping the benefits because of it.

Wow: The Science & The Data

To get consumers to buy from you time and time again you need a strategy, and **Wow** gives you exactly that. There are three parts to the **Wow** strategy that we can explore and validate with psychology:

1. Habit building: getting your consumers to habitually turn to you in their hour of need. Helping your consumers develop a customer lifetime habit with you.

2. What goes into building a habit, and how you can make the process easy.

3. The rules of thumb we use and how you can create your own positive rule sets to encourage engagement.

Wow helps you become a staple in your consumers' lives. Let's take a peek at how habits are formed and how you can trigger habits more efficiently. Habits save our brains effort. We do less work and place lower cognitive demand on our minds by forming rules of thumb. And habits form a big part of rules of thumb.

If we do certain things over and over again, and we don't create an automatic process to deal with it, we're wasting cognitive capacity—and the brain doesn't like wasting precious resources on repetitive tasks. So if the incoming information is the same, and the task is the same, the brain starts to develop a habit to cut down on resource usage.

In 2007, Wood and Neal proposed that we outsource our control over behavioural response to certain cues to habits[6]. They suggested habits can form in two ways:

1. **Repetition.** You see X happen, so you do Y. X is a behavioural cue and Y is a behavioural routine. The more you do the cue-

---

6 Wood, W. and Neal, D.T. (2007) 'A new look at habits and the habit-goal interface' *Psychol Rev* 114(4) pp843–63

Hack The Buyer Brain

routine dance, the stronger your brain associates the two, until eventually you don't need to think about things; when the cue happens, you just act.

2.   **Reward.** Sometimes there isn't just a cue and a routine; at the end of the routine there may be a reward. The reward changes the game because it gives us a reason to do the routine. We like rewards, so we'll do the routine more to get more rewards.

Interestingly, you can teach habits, which means you can build habitual associations with certain things. One of the best examples of this comes from Claude C Hopkins[7].

Hopkins made brushing teeth popular: he made clean teeth a habit. Thank you, Mr Hopkins, I am ever so grateful for the habit of fresh breath. Hopkins was hired by Pepsodent in the early 1900s to boost sales. Within ten years, he took the majority of Americans from not brushing their teeth frequently (if at all) to a nation of clean mouths— which is pretty amazing.

Here's how he did it: he put together an advert in which he primed a cue, then told his audience what the routine was, and specified the reward.

1.   **The cue.** Hopkins taught people that the 'film' on teeth (you can feel it when you've not brushed them at the end of the day), was bad for you. He told people to check by running your tongue over your teeth.

2.   **The routine.** If they could feel the film, people needed to brush their teeth with Pepsodent, which is minty and makes your mouth feel fresh—and it removes the film.

3.   **The reward** was the clean minty tingle—a good sign.

I know that I have Hopkins to thank for the clean minty tingle I crave in the mornings and evenings. Despite never having seen those original adverts, the habit has been passed on from generation to generation. Hopkins created a habit by pointing out the cue, providing a routine, and then making the reward really clear.

But now we're a little more savvy about marketing messages getting us into habits we may or may not need, can we still affect behaviour?

---

7 Hopkins, C.C. (2014) *Scientific Advertising*, Merchant Books

The answer is *yes*. It's a little harder, but if you want your consumers to turn directly to you in their time of need, you must create habits. In particular, you want your customer to be in the habit of coming to you first, rather than to your competition. Build positive loyalty and associations between you and the problems you're helping people solve.

According to Stephen Wendel[8], all you need to do to build a habit is:

1. Identify a routine that will be repeated dozens of times.
2. Identify a reward that's meaningful to the consumer.
3. Identify a clear and simple cue.
4. Make sure your consumer knows about the cue, routine, and reward.
5. Make sure the consumer can and wants to undertake the action.
6. Release the cue.
7. Help make the routine happen.
8. Immediately reward the user if they do the routine.
9. Repeat steps 6–8.

It's easiest if cues are tied to other events (so they piggy-back off an established routine) or happen at a specific time of day, every day or week. Hopkins used each of these nine steps to get the majority of Americans into the habit of using Pepsodent.

The easiest way for *you* to create a habit is with content. If you release valuable, meaningful content your audience wants to see, do it as regularly as possible so you form a habit for consumption. That way, you create habitual associations for people to engage with your content. The more engagement you get, the more likely people are to purchase, and the better your customer lifetime value will be. The more often someone sees your content, the more they use your products, the more they'll like your products.

In other words, putting a habit in place will also help consumers be more satisfied with your products. This is because of the 'mere exposure' effect cognitive bias, which we touched on earlier.

In 1968 Zajonc proposed the mere exposure effect with a nifty

---

8 Wendel, S. (2013) *Designing for Behavior Change*, O'Reilly Media Inc.

little study[9]. He showed how we have a tendency to develop more positive feelings towards objects the more we're exposed to them. To demonstrate this, he showed participants ten Chinese-like characters for two seconds.

Some participants only saw the characters once, while others saw them multiple times, up to 25 times each. Then he asked them to guess whether they had a positive or negative connotation. There was a direct correlation between how often someone saw the characters and how positive they thought they were. People liked the ones they saw more often.

But I don't expect you to just believe a study done in the late 60s: this effect has been replicated and investigated more than 200 times since then. The effect isn't limited to visual input, either—it works for auditory and food stimuli, too. By showing up with good quality content and getting your consumers to use their products more often, you're priming people to like you.

Sometimes there are obstacles in the way to creating habits and positive associations. Adam Ferrier suggests you do one of two things to get past obstacles: increase motivation or increase ease[10]. He suggests we can change and adapt behaviour if the consumer is motivated to change, and that it's relatively easy to do if conditions are right.

If motivation or ease aren't in place, customers will fall at the obstacles. Motivating action is complicated because humans are a bit of a complicated mess when it comes to motivation and emotion—but to increase motivation we can look at individual incentives and social norms. The greater the incentive is to do something, the more likely we are to do it. So you can ask yourself, how much incentive is there for your consumer to do what you want them to do?

Think about rewards and punishments. Will your consumers get a great reward if they use your product or engage with your content? Does the reward outweigh the punishment of *not* using it? If not, they probably won't do it.

But what about social norms? We are heavily influenced by what

9 Zajonc, R.B. (1968) 'Attitudinal effects of mere exposure', *Journal of Personality and Social Psychology*, 9(2, Pt.2), 1–27
10 Ferrier, A. (2014) *The Advertising Effect: How to Change Behaviour*, OUP Australia & New Zealand

other people are doing and how we may be perceived by others. So ask yourself: if your customers do this thing you're asking them to do, how will it make them look to their peers? If it's going to influence people's perception negatively, your customers probably won't do what you want them to do. But if it's going to make them look amazing and heighten their social standing, they'll be highly motivated to comply.

What about ease? As Ferrier points out, ease can be tricky to nail down. Mostly, it's the combination of ability and opportunity. If someone has the ability to do something and they're highly motivated, they will probably do it. But if they don't have the ability to do it, they need to acquire that ability, which makes it hard for them to do.

So the question to ask yourself is: are your consumers able to do what you want them to do? Or is it hard for them? How can you help them improve their abilities and make it easy?

When it comes to opportunity, this can be a timing factor, but it can also be about helping people create an opportunity themselves. Take healthy eating: it's easy to eat good stuff at home because you have the opportunity to prepare healthy food. It's much harder to do it on the road because the opportunity's not there—or it's far easier to grab some junk food.

Look at whether or not your consumers can actually do what you're asking them to do.

Using these questions lets you troubleshoot the habit you're trying to put in place. If consumers have high motivation and it's very easy to do, it will be possible for them to do what you're asking of them. If both are low, they probably won't do it. And if you have the one or the other, they *might* do it—but you could make it easier for them.

Netflix is an example of a company doing this dance really well: it's nailed the ease and motivation battle and made using the service so simple consumers have almost no desire to stop watching shows. They've just made it all incredibly easy. As a result, their customer leaving rate (churn) is less than 9 per cent[11].

Netflix keeps the consumer consuming, and make it incredibly simple to do so. They know that if their customers continue to watch,

---

11 Patel, N. (n.d.) How Netflix maintains a low churn rate by keeping customers engaged and watching. https://neilpatel.com/blog/how-netflix-maintains-low-churn/

they'll stick around. For them, everything is about the consumer's customer lifetime value.

Customer lifetime value is a vital baseline for your business, and it's the one statistic that you should always improve. Increase it by providing an awesome experience, adding value, and showing you care about your customers.

These same tactics help you create habits in your customers, increasing consumption and helping customers enjoy your product more. It's a win-win for you and for the consumer: you get your profits and they get a meaningful relationship based on value.

The Brain Hack

Humans are a messy collection of emotions and habits. Our brains are lazy, so if we do something over and over again, they create an automatic process to deal with it. A habit. This saves cognitive energy, which increases our chances of survival.

But the buyer brain doesn't just want an easy life: it also wants pleasure. For a short while after buying something, customers are super-happy, which is the ideal time to offer them another product or service. Leave it too long, and that dopamine wears off letting buyer's remorse set in.

Hack Your Buyer's Brain

You can hack your buyer's brain by encouraging your customers to build habits for both amazing customer lifetime value and happier customers. Delivering a wonderful **Wow** experience throughout the buying process—but especially during that dopamine high—keeps consumers happy.

Providing plenty of regular, useful, valuable content helps build a habit that keeps your customers coming back for more:

1. Identify a routine that will be repeated dozens of times.
2. Identify a reward that's meaningful to the consumer.
3. Identify a clear and simple cue.
4. Ensure your consumer knows the cue, routine, and reward.
5. Make sure the consumer can and wants to do the action.
6. Release the cue.
7. Help make the routine happen.
8. Immediately reward the user if they do the routine.
9. Repeat steps 6–8.

CONTENT

CHAPTER 7: Content—Sales By Stealth

"The royal road to a man's heart is to talk to him about the things he treasures most."

~ Dale Carnegie

CHAPTER 7: Content—Sales By Stealth

Content: The Principle & The Problem

Content marketing is defined as:

> *'Marketing that tries to attract customers by distributing informational content potentially useful to the target audience, rather than by advertising products and services in the traditional way.'*[1]

Certainly, that's been the general gist of it since at least 1732[2]. Bizarrely, it was Benjamin Franklin who gave us one of our first examples—the annual *Poor Richard's Almanack*, which he created to promote his printing business.

Since then, throughout the 1800s and 1900s there have been some exemplary forms of content marketing, such as the *Michelin Guide*,

1 Blackman, A. (2016) 'What Is Content Marketing?' Envato tutsplus https://business.tutsplus.com/tutorials/what-is-content-marketing--cms-26276
2 Pulizzi, J. (2016) 'The History of Content Marketing' Content Marketing Institute https://contentmarketinginstitute.com/2016/07/history-content-marketing/

originally launched by Michelin to encourage people to take their cars out and find lodgings while travelling[3]. The introduction of their star system in 1926 made it easy for motorists to understand the quality of places to stay or eat in.

Now, having a Michelin star is the mark of an exemplary restaurant, and fine dining establishments strive to attain star status. The guide is still in production and ranks more than '40,000 establishments in over 24 territories across three continents, and more than 30 million *Michelin Guides* have been sold worldwide'. Not bad for a guide that was originally created to get people excited about driving their cars.

Since 2004, we've seen content marketing as we know it today surface: blogs, videos, podcasts, webinars, and the like. Mostly these are endeavours from businesses to create some useful content that thinly disguises an attempt to sell services and products. Yes, I do sound disgruntled! And that's because most businesses don't do content very well. There has been a steady increase in the number of businesses creating content merely as an SEO strategy to rank and get traffic through the door, so they can sell at consumers (interestingly, these are often the businesses that say content marketing doesn't work). An unfortunate side-effect of this trend is content saturation: a flood of content into the market that makes life noisy. This may put most businesses at a disadvantage, but it actually offers a fantastic opportunity for you to differentiate your business from your competition.

Content marketing is no longer just a method of feeding the Google machine; it's now crucial to the consumer lifecycle. The role of content marketing is changing. It's not just a lead-generation tool anymore. It's now a way for your consumer to get to know you, educate themselves, and choose the best option possible. And, as we've covered in the previous chapters, content marketing is a fabulous way to ensure you engage and nurture your consumer through their buying process.

Content is vital in the **Attract** phase, the **Nurture** phase, the **Sell** phase and the **Wow** phase. There's no place that content doesn't have a home in your customer journey. The question is no longer whether or

---

3 'History of the Michelin Guide' Michelin https://guide.michelin.com/sg/history-of-the-michelin-guide-sg

not you should provide content—that's a given, and consumers expect it. Rather, it's what kind of content you need to produce and where you need to put it.

The other problem with content marketing is that noise issue. Since 2017, the number of pages viewed on WordPress websites started to decline for the first time ever[4]. That, of course, has an impact on the amount of time people spend on your site. This in itself is a problem, because the longer consumers spend on your site, the better.

According to Wolfgang Digital's 2017 study, if you increase the time consumers spend on your site by 16 per cent, you can increase conversions by 10 per cent[5]. So the key here is to help people find you in all that noise, then encourage them to stick around. That is, of course, where your content comes in.

Good content engages consumers and encourages them to stay on your website, getting to know you. The issue is getting found in the first place. Shouting your way through all that noise is hard.

This is generally when a decent SEO strategy comes in handy. It's more important than ever to use a strategy that will get you to the first page of Google for the content you want to rank for. Pop over to Google and ask it to show you all the best strategies for ranking, and it will give you roughly 211,000,000 results. (The irony of searching on Google for how to rank in searches on Google amuses me.)

The fundamental problem is you can't game the system anymore. Google makes every effort to keep the inner machinations of its algorithm shrouded in secrecy. What we *do* know is the algorithm is clever and tough. I am deliberately referencing Google here because Google is still the champion when it comes to share of online traffic.

Wolfgang Digital showed that for their study participants, a full 40 per cent of traffic came *just* from organic Google traffic[6]. Combine their Google pay-per-click traffic (24 per cent) and direct traffic (17 per cent), and Google alone accounts for over 80 per cent of the traffic that goes to websites.

---

4 Rayson, S. (2018) 'Content Trends 2018: BuzzSumo Research Report' BuzzSumo
5 'E-commerce Report 2017', Wolfgang Digital www.wolfgangdigital.com/uploads/case-studies/Wolfgang_Digital_2017_E-commerce_KPI_Benchmarks_Study.pdf
6 'E-commerce Report 2017', Wolfgang Digital

Traffic is only part of the story, though. What about revenue? Looking at the revenue generators, Google still dominates. It brings in 41 per cent of the revenue for organic traffic, and 25 per cent for cost-per-click. Social only brings in 1 per cent, which is five times less then email at 5 per cent. Bing brings in a paltry 2 per cent. The other search engines are getting better, but Google wins. Dominate Google and you dominate it all.

Ranking, then, is definitely a battle you want to fight and win. And once you have the consumer there on your site, getting them to stay is your next objective. Creating content addresses both these problems, surely? Content has to be the solution, right?

Well, here you encounter the third problem, the one we raised right at the beginning of this chapter: not all content is created equal, and most of it is pretty pants.

As my lovely friend Vicky Fraser says: 'We are drowning in a deluge of crap content. Everyone has jumped on the bandwagon, thrown blogs up without a f*** given, and now the crap is coming back down to drown us when we look for meaningful information.'

I couldn't have said it better. That's not to say the trend of content creation is a bad thing—it's great that consumers have challenged businesses to provide better information and experiences. No, the issue lies mostly with how businesses create content. Generally, the plan for content creation starts by reverse engineering what you have to offer and finding things you can talk about that link to what you offer. So you map out what you want the consumer to do, then create the content to fit. It's an easy trap to fall into, but it's still a trap.

Instead, find out what consumers need in the moment, then adapt and tweak your plan to ensure you cover the appropriate messaging.

The current definition of content marketing is: 'distributing informational content that is potentially useful'. I'd change this to: 'distributing informational content of *value*'.

Consumers are discerning and they won't waste their time on information that doesn't meet their needs—only 9 per cent of consumers stay on a page that doesn't immediately match what they're looking for; the other 91 per cent leave[7]. Additionally, consumers dislike

---

7 Google (2011) *Winning the Zero Moment of Truth.*

content that is overly salesy. You've probably heard the statistic that says 70 per cent of the buying journey is complete before consumers reach out to salespeople. Well, the statistic has become a little warped over time. The research comes from Sirius Decisions, and the actual quote is: '67 per cent of the buying journey is now done digitally'[8]. This just means consumers prefer researching first before being sold to. Consumers do not want to be sold to, that is a fact; but they do want information. And, once they have some information, they are happy to chat with salespeople to get more information.

Which brings us to an important distinction—content is not sales. Content is valuable information, and good content is conversion focused, but that doesn't mean it's salesy.

Conversion means the user performed the action you wanted them to do. That could be clicking to the next blog post, signing up for more information, clicking a button, or even purchasing. Conversion doesn't exclusively mean purchase.

Your content should be conversion focused; it should be getting the consumer to do something specific. It should also add value and provide information to them so they're a better prospect for you to work with. Ideally, your content always gets your consumers ready for that next step in their journey, whatever it is. Don't get caught up in selling in all of your content.

Instead, provide valuable information they care about that will add value—and focus on converting them to the next step in the journey. That's the role of good content within the customer journey. If you have good content, you'll keep consumers on your site longer, which will help you get conversions.

In turn, by providing the content consumers want, you should rank well in search engine results. It's all about the win-win!

Content: The Solution

Now we're clear about creating conversion-focused content, how do you make sure you create the kind of content your consumer wants to see? To best answer this question, think about what Google really, really wants to do. Any search engine's function is to provide the best

8 Heuer, M (2013) 'Three Myths of the "67 Percent" Statistic', Sirius Decisions

information possible for our needs. If it doesn't provide you with relevant, personalised information in your moment of need, you'll go off and find a better search engine. The entire purpose for giants like Google is to provide you with what you want at the click of a button, no matter how silly the request.

Google never judges you, it just answers you to the best of its ability, no matter what. In order to protect you as the user from the businesses out there that just want to sell and aren't bothered about how well they've answered the question, Google has super-duper algorithms that analyse content, keep track of how engaged users are once they click through, and generally just keep an eye on things to make sure it's fulfilling its prime directive: providing the right information to the user.

If you want to try to game the system, be my guest. The algorithms change so often it's more than a full-time job keeping up with them. Instead, your best way to rank is to simply be relentlessly helpful. At every stage in the buyer journey, the consumer has questions. Those questions are gold. Simply answer these questions for consumers and add value, always. This strategy is beautifully explained in my good friend Marcus Sheridan's book, *They Ask, You Answer*[9]. The basic premise is: you pour all your content energy into creating awesome content that answers the questions your audience is asking about your industry, your products, or your services.

This strategy helped Marcus survive the recession of 2008 as the owner of a pool company, River Pools and Spas. While businesses were shutting down around him left, right and centre, Marcus focused on being relentlessly helpful and explicitly answering the questions consumers were asking. He built trust and engagement with his audience by providing honest and thoughtful answers to five categories of questions:

- Cost/Price
- Problems
- Comparisons
- Reviews
- Best of/Top 5

---

9 Sheridan, M. (2017) *They Ask, You Answer.* John Wiley & Sons

Marcus's honesty and breadth and depth of knowledge impressed enough consumers that River Pools and Spas not only survived one of the most daunting and chaotic times for small businesses in recent history, it's now the most-visited pool website in the US, and possibly globally. These categories allow you to provide content for the vast majority of questions people are asking, while still allowing you to move them onto the next step in their customer journey.

We also advise you to answer questions in two more categories:

- What is
- How to

These are the topics consumers are looking for help with. Validate this advice with a little research into search volumes and you're onto a winning content strategy. Be there providing honest information for what customers need in that moment. If you do so with good content, you'll fix the page-dwell time issue, and the ranking issue.

Don't stop there. Make sure you build trust in places you may not yet have it. Another good friend of mine, Russ Haworth, recently joined me for a tipple of gin and a spot of customer-journey planning in my office. While deep into his journey, we troubleshooted his content. I asked what his conversion focus was and he mentioned he didn't have many lead magnets, and that most of his content's calls to action were to meet with him. Being a financial planner, this made sense.

When I challenged the salesy feeling of a meeting, he countered that the meeting was not a sales pitch at all and was actually totally value-based. In the meeting, he takes people through their finances, investments, and pensions and gives them a red, amber or green score. He then gives people a plan to execute. If they're interested, they ask him about his services and he follows up.

But Russ isn't always right for them, so he's careful to use the meeting to build a relationship, *not* to sell. His consumers, however, have no idea that's the case. Their assumption is that he will be selling to them, so they shy away from a meeting.

The solution we came up with was to offer a checklist as the main call to action instead. The checklist allows consumers to self-assess, and they can then choose red, amber, or green. The information he usually gives in the face-to-face meeting is then sent in a series of content pieces to help people understand their financial status. This way, he builds trust and engagement.

At the end of that process he can ask again for the meeting, and by this point he's already added value so they trust him more.

This process is part of dissecting what consumers are asking for help with and asking yourself, 'What are they doing?', 'What are they thinking?', and 'What are they feeling?' at each point. When you look at Russ's calls to action you realise consumers feel wary, and they want to get the information first without having to speak to someone. Once they trust you, people respond more favourably to the request for a meeting. By creating content like this, you build trust, engagement, and a relationship, while being relentlessly helpful.

Go even further, though. Use the content you're creating for the upfront journey to help engage and nurture your existing database of leads and customers. If the content is helpful and non-salesy, use it to keep your audience's excitement levels up. Distribute the content to your list as you create it and automate the distribution. We call the process of automating nurture content a long-term nurture campaign. The goal with this campaign is to send content out to people to do the following:

- Nurture and continue to build relationships
- Track engagement
- Segment

Depending on the relationship you have with your list, we suggest sending content out weekly if your creation schedule allows it. Weekly is the easiest way to make consuming content habitual (as we touched on in Chapter 6)

If you're worried about how often that is, remember the frequency of sending simply depends on the expectations you set. If you tell people you'll send them valuable content every week and they agree to that, you're not upsetting anyone. If you tell them you'll send it monthly, then you email them every three days, you'll upset some people.

Sending a nice mix of content out on a specific schedule helps keep your audience engaged and excited to hear from you. You'll build your reputation with them and provide valuable answers to their questions.

That is the nurturing and relationship building part of the customer journey. The part of this strategy I get most excited about, however, is tracking engagement and segmenting. By tracking the content people are engaging with, you can see what your audience is most interested in. This in itself is invaluable because you'll discover there is some content you're convinced is going to work that simply doesn't, and other content you're amazed people are so interested in. That's the nature of the content game.

You can validate with projection data and search volumes as much as you like, but nothing beats cold, hard engagement statistics. This is a positive feedback loop and you'll be able to validate and adjust your course so you're always providing relevant and consumable information. While you're tracking engagement, segment your audience based on that engagement. Behaviour always provides you with insights consumer surveys won't be able to give you. When you segment based on behaviour, you'll uncover what people are really struggling with, and which products and services might be of interest to them. Then set a threshold for engagement. The threshold is there to tell you about those people who are really super-engaged with a certain topic.

For instance, if you're a financial planner you might send out content on broad financial health, pensions, and investments. If your consumers engage with three pieces of investment content, chances are they're very interested in investments and probably need some help. Automate the threshold counting so it notifies you or your sales team, or triggers an automated campaign to get in touch and offer more personalised content.

You can also start the sales process for investments. This is behavioural selling. You know what they're interested in, and if you have a product that matches their interest over a certain threshold, they'll be interested in hearing more about it.

You can then use each of these segments for future campaigns. If you're feeling particularly fancy you can trigger retargeting to them based on their engagements and follow them around the internet with helpful information. Adapt and change the calls to action on your site as your visitors' requirements and engagements change and develop. Always keep it personal.

The rad thing about this strategy is you never sell in the long-term nurture. It's pure value-add. You only ever sell based on what consumers are engaging with. Use the information you gather to feed back into your site and adapt your retargeting strategies. This makes your content super-personalised and relevant, which is exactly what consumers are crying out for and demanding from businesses. This kind of content is the backbone of your customer journey.

While lifecycle marketing is the framework you build your customer journey around, it's the content that keeps everything together. You need content in each and every stage of your journey, not just for ranking and the sales process, but for engagement, nurture, customer lifetime value, and behavioural selling. Content makes it all possible, one engagement at a time.

Content: Real Life

Content marketing makes sense for a lot of businesses, but for some of the bricks-and-mortar businesses it can seem like a completely esoteric concept. If you run a brick-and-mortar business and can't see how content could help you, let me introduce you to Gillies and Mackay (G&M), a second-generation family business.

Cara Mackay is the managing director, and she's a woman on a mission. Ever since I met Cara I knew she was awesome; she's an incredible force to be reckoned with and has channelled that force into G&M. Cara shares her story here, and I've left it in her own words because she is so fabulously Scottish and authentic, that it would be a shame to change a single thing.

'In May 2015 a "Masterclass in Content Marketing", run by Learning Everyday with Chris Marr, enrolled 12 new students for a six-month programme. I was one of those students.

'I had been roped into the workshop by Col Gray. We'd met at a previous workshop and created a long-lasting friendship. Col is a graphic designer and branding specialist. He did an amazing job with the G&M branding, and I bought him beer.

'So far so good, but Col had asked if I'd be interested in the content marketing workshop. Being me, I asked, "Can we have beers after?" He said OK, and the deal was done.

'Roll ahead to the first masterclass with the phenomenal Chris Marr and I'm not 100 per cent sure of this guy. Firstly, he is young and handsome—there must be a catch right? Ah yes, there it is. He's talking shite. I'm fresh out of uni with a 2:1 honours degree in business management—marketing being my straight A subject for four years—and I knew everything there was to know.

'Or did I? Chris had started the masterclass with a discussion about industry-specific issues—what are they? What do we complain about in our industries? What do our customers complain about? And, worse, what do our customers not know about? One of the other students, Gordon Mathie, had a massive light-bulb moment and declared, 'I don't want to become the Betamax of my industry!' I'm dead young so had no idea what he was talking about, but it sounded powerful. I got the gist that someone was really good at something, but nobody knew that was the case.

'HELLO!! G&M alarm bells ringing!

'That was us. We make the best sheds in the world. The two men who created G&M are an incredible force—honest and hard-working men—just like our sheds. They are also both still operational. John Mackay is my dad and Grant Gillies is my uncle. John is a horticultural graduate and knows his wood better than anyone—he literally lives and breathes it. Grant spent his trade in Canada lumbering log cabins in the northern hemisphere—Grant can build anything.

'BUT. Unless your neighbour happens to get one or you're passing by our precariously placed workshop tucked away on a fruit farm, you'll never find us or know there's an alternative to mass-produced shite sheds. Until now.

'G&M never really entertained traditional advertising, and after years of being f**** over by the *Yellow Pages*, the BT phone book and *The Courier*, I'd eventually told them all to shove off. This means that for the past three years G&M's entire marketing strategy was and still is based on content marketing, and content marketing alone.

'You can learn a lot of lessons in three years.

1. Appreciate what it is that you do and if you do not know exactly what that is then content marketing isn't going to work for you. This is an all-in commitment to your product or service or

offering. If you don't believe in it, no-one else will.

2. Open your mind! No, you don't know everything—there is so much unlearning to be done before you can move forward.

3. Accept help, accept other professions, especially for things like branding, video-editing, publishing and websites. That's not your job, and the sooner you admit it and pay someone else the quicker it gets done right and the quicker you get on with your own work!

4. You will be faced with a turmoil of doubt. Especially from those around you, people that don't get it, and people who haven't a clue why you'd spend all this time pursuing something that doesn't make sense to them. But, worst of all, you'll face internal doubt. Being able to see past this and focus on the fundamental principles of why content marketing exists will be your success. It's not instant, and typically it takes years (three to be exact in our case) to reap the full benefits of what you sow.'

And Cara has certainly done that. Over the course of the last three years she's completed the Content Success Formula course created by Marcus Sheridan and Chris Marr. Using the principles she learned in that course, and the philosophy from *They Ask You Answer*, she made over 100 targeted videos and wrote 200 blogs, and she's still going. Each piece of content answers specific questions and helps position G&M as the experts they are.

The numbers speak for themselves: the 2018 end-of-year operational profit was £95,000; the 2019 end-of-year operational profit was £225,000. Content marketing has helped G&M become visible, it's helped them communicate who they are and why their sheds are the best in world, it's got them in front of the right consumers, and it's got them a rabid base of Sheddies—the shed fans who know their spruce from their Scandinavian pine.

There is one more thing that content marketing has done for Cara, but I can't promise it will do the same for you. Cara and Chris ended up falling in love, combining their families, and having a baby: the adorable Luna. It's a story with a happy ending, and you won't find more deserving content fanatics out there.

Content: The Science & The Data

There is a lot of data behind the power of content marketing, and we've had 17 years to prove its efficiency. And while there are many different ways to create amazing information, and hundreds of companies like Gillies and Mackay that have succeeded with the strategy, one thing hasn't changed: Google is the gatekeeper to success. If you can't get past Google, you're not going to succeed.

There are, however, some specific ways you can get ahead:

1. Answer the questions consumers are asking
2. Get people to spend time on your site
3. Encourage people to move to the next step or page
4. Optimise your pages for SEO and track their rankings
5. Ensure headings, subheadings, and images are SEO-friendly
6. Your meta descriptions are crucial, as is your page title
7. Encourage users to come back to your site if possible

There are many more tips and tricks you can use, but did you notice only three of the seven I listed are even vaguely technical? That's because the behaviour your consumers display reinforces what Google decides to do with you.

Number 7 is particularly important, and if you look at the Wolfgang Digital 2016 report you'll notice that Google and email between them are a responsible for a full 73 per cent of revenue[10]. It's also fascinating that websites with great SEO strategies had a higher average order value—so if you nail your SEO you have the potential to earn more per sale. Since 2014, the average order conversion rate has risen by 10 per cent, and its value has increased by 25 per cent. This is despite social referral traffic and shares declining by a full 50 per cent since 2015. So while there's a lot of doom and gloom about how the internet is cluttered, if you can cut through the noise you have the potential to reap some serious benefits.

As all this change is happening, purchase journeys are getting longer. In a 12-month period from 2016 to 2017, journey lengths

---

10 'E-commerce KJPI Benchmarks 2016', Wolfgang Digital www.wolfgangdigital.com/uploads/general/eComKPI2016-Public2.pdf

grew by a full 12 per cent[11]. This means it's taking significantly longer for consumers to convert. If you have no focus on building a journey that helps consumers convert, it's time to get worried, because your consumers might not stick around long enough to buy from you.

Journeys are also getting more convoluted, and there are more touch points now from different channels. On average, it takes 2.77 touch points to get a conversion[12]. Last-click attribution models won't tell you the whole story, so what's a business to do? The biggest mindset change we need to make is to understand that the journey is no longer linear; it doesn't stick on one platform, or one mode of communication. The journey is cumulative.

Focus on crafting an experience that is fluid across platforms, provides personalised information, and keeps people coming back for more and spending longer when they do. That's what we call a sticky journey: sites people like to hang around on, emails people like to open and, ultimately, journeys that sell more.

So, what's a sticky journey? Well, according to the 2018 Buzzsumo Content Report, it's a journey that focuses on building authority and loyalty[13]. It's not about the amount of content produced, but the quality of content in the journey. It's not necessarily even hot, trendy content that matters.

The report found that evergreen content is consistently popular and builds reputation. A sticky journey includes long-tail, high-quality content (answering full questions, rather than focusing on shorter keywords or owning subtopics). Two sites that exemplify this and have continuously bucked downward trends are the *Harvard Business Review* and *The Economist*. Rather than jumping on the trend bandwagon and producing as many clickbait articles as possible, these two sites spent more time producing well-crafted, quality content. They've seen their shares rise, and their audience has grown because of it.

The thread running through all this is to go back to basics. Build your audience and create more direct ways of getting your content to people. Yes, I mean email lists. Social reach is continually decreasing,

11 'E-commerce Report 2017', Wolfgang Digital
12 'E-commerce Report 2017', Wolfgang Digital
13 Rayson, S. (2018) 'Content Trends 2018: BuzzSumo Research Report' BuzzSumo

and as that happens you need to take control of what you can.

For instance, 52 per cent of consumers still find the sites they're looking for via search—so own your SEO. The other thing you can own is your database: email is not dead. If you have something new and you tell your list about it, on average 20 per cent of them will open that email. Tweet about it and only 1–3 per cent of them will see the tweet.

Email also enjoys the highest average order value of all channels which is, in part, because those on your list are your loyal consumers. You've had the chance to build authority with them, so by all means create content that gets new traffic onto the site—but share it again with your email list to really get the system working.

Remember: content is the backbone of your customer journey, so give the creation, distribution, and automation of it the reverence it deserves.

The Brain Hack

Our super-efficient brains are brilliant at tuning out irrelevant details - like the content white noise flooding the internet - and we actively avoid pushy sales messages because they're a threat to our precious resources (time and cold, hard cash).

We've evolved to pay attention only to information that helps us survive and thrive. So if you want to create content that'll get you noticed, you need to...

Hack Your Buyer's Brain

Focus on being relentlessly helpful and explicitly answer the questions consumers are asking. Build trust and engagement by creating content that honestly and thoughtfully answers questions in the following categories:

- Cost/Price
- Problems
- Comparisons
- Reviews
- Best of/Top 5
- What is
- How to

CHAPTER 8: Create Your Customer Journey

"It is good to have an end to journey toward, but it is the journey that matters in the end."

~ Ursula K. Le Guin

CHAPTER 8: Create Your Customer Journey

The Customer Journey: The Principle & The Problem

It's easy to imagine the brain as this all-knowing ultimate controller, moving us through our lives with purpose and direction. There's a stark sense of irony that the brain makes you believe the conscious mind is more in control than it actually is.

Unfortunately, the brain is not the machine we, and it, think it is. It certainly isn't in as much conscious control as we'd like it to be. It's an organ that's evolved simply to keep us alive. We made it this far because of how its quirks and eccentricities have incrementally given us survival advantage.

In the same way we design for desired outcomes, the brain only ever had one purpose: to survive. Every day we use systems that have evolved over thousands of years to merely increase our chances of survival, and every day we hack them. That hacking allows us to outperform every other species on the planet so far (although I'd still rather be a cat). But, as we've seen, it's not without cost. We make mistakes.

Thankfully, technology has progressed to the point that we can see those mistakes. We can see how the brain is hacking itself, and if we can see it, we can measure it. Because we can measure it, we're starting to understand it. Our new understanding gives us huge leverage to change the way we go about helping consumers and motivating people.

Unfortunately, the world of academia can make all the golden insights completely inaccessible to the average business owner. My hope is this book has brought you one step closer to clarity on why you should craft a behavioural experience. And I hope you now better understand how it all fits together.

We know consumers are desperate for acknowledgement and understanding, and we know they demand a personalised experience. And using the formula we created we also know that:

experience = [personalisation x (engagement points)] + perception.

We've got some clarity on the perception, we've got the engagement points, and we know we need to personalise them. Lifecycle marketing gives us the framework we need to achieve a crafted experience. Behaviour allows us to understand how the consumer perceives that experience at each point, and why we do the odd things we do. And finally, content provides the substance to add value. Content allows us to structure the process in such a way that we strategically use each step of the journey that the consumer goes through.

Those three ingredients—lifecycle marketing, behaviour, and content—allow you to craft behavioural customer journeys, and the interaction those journeys create generates experience.

When you're crafting a behavioural experience, the interplay of behaviour, lifecycle marketing, and content allow us to provide what the consumer wants. They allow us to build a relationship with the consumer while adding value.

Relationships have always been a requirement for successful sales, it's just been easy to forget that in a digital world where everything is so instantly accessible and yet so isolated. The consumer wants a journey, they want a relationship, and they want it on their terms. This hasn't changed since the beginning of trade—it's simply that before now, the consumer never realised exactly how much power they have. It's up to you to step up and give people what they want.

This, of course, can be totally overwhelming. Even with the lifecycle marketing framework, putting it all together can feel intimidating. I've spent the last four years creating behavioural customer journeys, and I've found that most successful ones all look the same. It doesn't matter what industry or which commercial group you're targeting, the foundational blocks are identical. This makes sense, because there is an underlying common thread: *humans*.

You're designing for humans, which means the prime drivers will be incredibly similar. This flies in the face of what some self-styled gurus in the industry tell you: it's simply not as complicated as it's made out to be. The lifecycle marketing framework is the same everywhere. The layout in which you use that behavioural journey is the same. The only thing that's different is the way you optimise it for your business and your consumers.

The Customer Journey: The Solution

Below is the framework that we have been developing and implementing for our customers. This structure turns the concepts we have covered, and the flywheel at the start of this chapter into a usable format you can steal, shown in Figure 6 overleaf.

Before we wrap up, let's take a look at this simple flow so you can take the essence of it and use it in your business.

Content

Starting from the left-hand side of the chart we have content (the orange blocks). This gets people's attention. You could drive ads to your content, or you could optimise for SEO. Your content can be blogs, videos, podcasts, physical books, etc. You name it, it's the stuff that brings people through your digital door.

Businesses that thrive with their content split it into at least two levels: basic and advanced. All the questions people ask you, any additional categories, etc. will fall into one of those two categories.

Content should always move people onto the next step, whether that's to get something of higher value (a lead magnet) or simply to move them to the next, slightly more advanced piece of content.

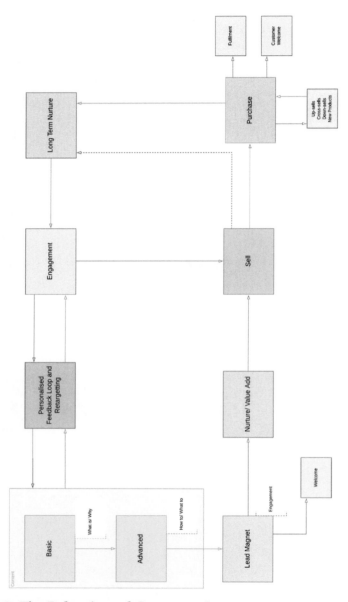

Figure 6: The Behavioural Customer Journey

Lead magnet

Next is the green square: the lead magnet. Consumers should take you up on some kind of lead magnet. This could be as simple as a higher level of engagement, like Coca-Cola's 'put your name on a bottle' campaign, test-driving a car, HubSpot's free CRM, or a checklist.

The important thing about the lead magnet is that it should move your consumer to the next step by adding value. It doesn't have to be a freebie, you could get people to visit a page you're tracking with pixels. Or your lead magnet could be a low-priced option of your standard product. Whatever you choose as a lead magnet, it's the next step to take unknown traffic to becoming known traffic.

Nurture and engagement

When a consumer gets a lead magnet, the nurturing starts. This is the all-important middle part of the journey where you help someone make a decision about what's right for them. It's also where you build a relationship and earn someone's trust.

You're gearing up to sell, so not only are you helping and adding huge amounts of value, you're also allowing the consumer to get to know you a little better. Most businesses fall flat here.

When I do lifecycle marketing assessments (or, as we prefer to call them, marketing therapy sessions), businesses understand **Attract**, and they understand **Sell**. However, their **Engage** strategy hardly ever has any substance to it, if it even exists at all. Improve your nurture campaigns and you'll help the consumer make the right choice for them and for you.

It's not too hard to put amazing **Nurture** in place. It simply means providing extra input and value on top of what the consumer opted in for, helping them get to their next step and bringing them closer to deciding what to do.

Sell

Now we arrive at the blue square of **Sell**: the point of sale where some businesses choke. It's hard to make sure you're not being overly salesy and putting the consumer off, or languishing at the other extreme of not being comfortable to sell at all and not making the offer clear.

Make sure your offer is tangible and clearly signalled, the reward is immediate and clear, and the choice is safe and certain. You'll fall foul of cognitive bias if you don't make your case explicit.

The purchase formula also comes into play at this point, so increase the perceived reward value and decrease the perceived cost. Whatever you do here, make it easy and congruent.

Welcome

After the sale, remember to welcome consumers on board. This isn't just about showing them the ropes—that's the job of on-boarding—this is all about making the effort to reach out to your brand-new customers and re-affirm that they're in the right place and they've made the right decision.

You can welcome people straight away at sign-up, if you like, so your brand-new leads can get to know you. How you do this depends on the type of lead magnet you offer and how your nurture is structured.

Nurture Post-Purchase

Post-purchase nurture is vital after the point of sale. This is the road to amazing customer lifetime value, where you ensure your consumer flies through any on-boarding smoothly. This is where you help them get stuck into using their purchase, and owning what they've bought.

Do this stage well and you'll move them to the status of loyal customer so they give you a glowing testimonial, and perhaps even some juicy referrals. Once you've checked in with your customer, ensure you have a way of offering them more, whether it's an up-sell, cross-sell, down-sell, or a new product.

Long-Term Nurture, Engagement/Short-Term Nurture

This is one of my favourite parts of the customer journey, for two reasons. First it's easy; and second, it's the area that I see makes the biggest difference to our clients and their consumers.

The long-term nurture kicks in after post-purchase to keep your consumers engaged and excited. It should also be triggered if a consumer doesn't convert, so you don't lose a potential customer before you've had a chance to build a relationship.

This is all great, but it's the long-term nurture and the engagement with the consumer that makes the magic happen. As your consumer engages with your long-term nurture, track them. We all need to learn how to read consumer behaviour. Their engagement, or lack thereof, tells you what they're most interested in. Segment your audience using that engagement, and set up thresholds that allow you to trigger specific sales sequences when you know a consumer is ready to purchase.

For example, if you send out three topics in the long-term nurture—topic A, B, and C—and you know each of those topics relates to products A, B, and C (because you've associated your products effectively) then you'll know that if the consumer engages with tons of information on topic C they are probably interested in or need help with C, so you can automatically offer them product C based on this engagement. This is amazing for conversion rates, but it's also amazing for personalised selling.

Feedback Loop

Don't stop there, though. This engagement will provide you with information as to how you should optimise your website's calls to action and layout for that consumer. As technology advances, we can adapt what consumers see on sites based on their individual requirements.

The problem is we very often don't open a feedback loop between the site, the calls to action, and engagement with content that's drip-fed to consumers. This feedback loop is vital, and you can use this information for retargeting and advertising for that specific consumer. Lack of data is not the problem; using it appropriately is.

Use the data you collect to inform the consumer journey. At every point in the journey, plan for customer actions and track and account for positive and negative behaviour, so you continually adapt what the consumer sees and experiences, across platforms, devices, and parts of their journey.

Looking at Figure 6, notice the colours. The green areas are labelled **Attract**, the purple areas are **Engage**, blue is **Sell**, and pink is **Wow**. We've pulled together lifecycle marketing and behaviour into a structure you can use to craft your customer's behavioural experience. Underlying this is your behavioural know-how. And its lifeblood is content. This structure weaves all three areas in this book into a tool you can use to create effective marketing systems.

Next Steps

So what do you do now? Download the Behavioural Customer Journey structure and some additional bonus resources at:

www.hackthebuyerbrain.com

You also have the option to book a free marketing therapy session. We'll sit down with you and figure out the solutions to your problems together, critique what you currently have, and send you off with a plan to make it happen.

It's our way of making sure you get ahead of the game. I'd also love for you to leave me a review and let me know what you're going to be taking away from this book.

Each journey starts with single step. Reading this book has been your first step in creating a behavioural experience your consumers will love. But now you need to take the second step: make it happen. You've got the know-how. You know about brain hacking, and you know how to hack the hacking. You have the structure, the clarity, and the science. You even know how other businesses have used customer lifecycle marketing and behavioural knowledge extremely successfully.

It's time to use that knowledge. Go out there and craft your own customer journey. Design it, and build it.

Your customers' experience depends on you.

Acknowledgements

Back home in South Africa, we often say it takes a village to raise a child. The same is certainly true of *Hack The Buyer Brain*. I am incredibly fortunate to have had the most phenomenal village help me raise this book.

To my family

Mom, Felicia, you both made me the woman I am today. The strength through adversity, the support to do anything, and the creativity to dream that you gave me is the best foundation a child could ask for. Thank you for the sacrifices you made, the million trips to the library when I wanted to "look up just one more thing...", and fielding a constant barrage of questions about life the universe and everything. You fostered my desire to learn, and that is the cornerstone of who I now am.

Glen, you are the Dad I never had. I am forever grateful for all the botties. Thank you for showing me what unconditional love really is. I love you.

Oskar, Draevon, and Jason, your fun has made everything easier to deal with—thank you.

Kayla-Leigh, your belief and determination to be who you really are is inspiring.

Jackie, your constant support and kindness is humbling, I couldn't ask for a better mother-in-law. Thank you so much for everything you have done for Mike and me.

Georg, you're a tough cookie, but that makes the nice things you say that much nicer, thank you for all your support.

Rory, Belinda, Cameron, and Leith, although I never got to have you in my life until much later, thank you for the relationship we have now built—I'm grateful to have you all in my life.

To my team

None of this would be possible without you. You're such awesome ninjas, and we all know I'd be completely lost without your support.

Mike, thank you for making sure I don't spend all the business money on cocktails. Mel, your ability to just get shit done never ceases to amaze me. Thank you for how hard you work. Your consistent growth to be the best ninja you can be is inspirational. Lucy, you're amazing. Thank you for your constant positivity and creativity. Your determination to make the best out of every situation is both refreshing and stimulating.

Beka, you've calmed me down, pepped me up, organised me, structured me, and generally kept me pointing in the right direction almost my entire life. This book would not have been possible without your unique skill in containing and directing my chaos.

Simon, thank you for your enthusiasm. You've been the best advocate. Thank you for reading the manuscript so quickly and running with its contents.

To my support network

This book would not have been possible without the resolute support of an amazing group of people and businesses. A special thank you to Keap. It was my original introduction to Infusionsoft by Keap that started this journey. The amazing Certified Partner community that Keap has built has nurtured and grown my business. Every case study used in this book is a success that is only possible because of Infusionsoft by Keap. So thank you to the founders, Scott Martineau, Eric Martineau and Clate Mask. Your software has made all of this possible—we are forever indebted to you for that.

Thank you to the indomitable Sarah Laws for being there from the very early days and giving me the spark to get started.

Melodie, you're my sister from a parallel universe. Thank you for your nudges, encouragement and love. Your support has meant the world.

Greg Jenkins, your wise words and support gave me strength when I got close to throwing the towel in.

Ahmed, Ramin, and Russ, our accountability group has kept my head on my shoulders. Thank you so much to all three of you for your succour.

Arfa, our crazy conversations are what sparked the desire to write the book. You're phenomenal, and your boldness gave me the mettle to get started.

Gareth Rifkin, your suggestions and excitement about the book got me through a rough patch in writing. Thank you.

Extra special glittery unicorn thanks to Chris Marr of the Content Marketing Academy. Your stoicism has steadied me. The community you have built is unlike any I have ever seen. I am so appreciative for the strength, motivation and growth you have given myself and the community members. A double thank you for the friendships I have made as a result of CMA. #CMA4LYF.

Cara, you're a dazzling, impressive magnificent woman. Your momness meant the world to me in a tough spot. What a complete legend you are.

Nic, you are so wise. Thank you for all your validation, kind words and constant support.

Ross, thank you for the confidence you gave me. It's spread through everything—you're so rad.

And dearest Debbie. You are the Anna to my Kendrick. You're the best cheerleader a girl could ask for. Thank you for your validation and challenging. You're absolutely amazing, and this book would be a shadow of itself without you.

To those that started it all

Seth Godin, you're a superstar. Seeing your talk at ICON 2014 showed me what Marketing could be. Your conversation with me after your talk inspired Automation Ninjas. This book would never have been a consideration if it weren't for you taking the time to chat. Thank you.

To Adam Ferrier, Daniel Kahneman, Thaler and Sunstein, Ariely, Knutson, and all your colleagues: thank you for the foundational research you have all done into how the brain really works. Your papers inspired this book.

Kevin and Vicki, you saw something in me that I couldn't. You stepped me outside my comfort zone and introduced me to the world. Thank you so much for making me take that step. Paul Tansey, your belief in me and in what we do is awe-inspiring. Thank you for the late nights, the phone calls, letting me share my crazy flow charts and running with the ideas that I nudge in front of you. All three of you have inspired a confidence in me that I can never lose. Thank you so much for what you've done.

To those that made this book possible

Cassandra, thank you for the gorgeous artwork. Your inspired vision has cascaded on to so much more.

Denise, my incredibly patient editor, you have been my saviour throughout the writing process. You made me sound good. Thank you.

Chris Brogan and Mike Finn, thank you for taking the time to read the book and give me honest feedback. Chris, your comments were harsh but fair—and when the rest of my village gave me a fat head, you helped me see areas that I could improve. I'm incredibly grateful for that.

Mike, Jennifer, and Vicky, I cannot thank you enough for Lanzarote. We got this book done because of that trip. Mike Browne, you are a constant inspiration—thank you. Jennifer Murgatroyd, thank you for helping me overcome one of the biggest hurdles in the writing process—believing in me. I cannot wait to read your book... And to the lovely Vicky Fraser. You've given me confidence, you've made this book look good, you've helped me tidy it up. I'm so glad I forced you to be my friend, and made you take a sheep home (sorry Joe). Thank you so much for all your encouragement, challenging, pushing, coaxing, and general awesomeness. You really have given me moxie.

To the menagerie

Salem, your incessant jumping on my keyboard has taught me how fragile the present is. Your battle (and triumph) with lymphoma was one of the hardest challenges we have faced, but you never let that stop you being my constant companion. Thank you for your late night support, your cuddles and purrs, and the lessons you have taught me about life. Naartjie and Nermal, your never ending silliness brightens every day. My life would be two dimensional with out all of you, my four legged friends, and I am incredibly privileged to be your guardian.

This book undoubtedly would have been published a lot faster without you, but it wouldn't have been as much fun to write.

To Mike, my long suffering husband

Finally, thank you to my phenomenal husband Mike. Your passion, encouragement, love and strength means everything to me. You are the ultimate companion, and you're not only my chosen partner for work, you're my chosen partner for life.

Thank you for the 2,417 morning teas you have made me (yes I worked it out). It's not just the tea that helps me get up in the morning, it's your happy bearded face too. Thank you for the other million cups of tea you supplied me with while writing this book, I wouldn't have made it past the first page without you.

Thank you for believing in me when I couldn't believe in myself, and for your unerringly stubborn support through my dark days. It's not easy living with a crazy person but you make it look like a breeze. There is no one else on the planet I'd rather inflict my craziness on.

Thank you for sharing my enthusiasm about the book, for your infuriating attention to detail, and for reading the same sentences 20 times for each change I made.

Who knew that a birthday party in a dingy pub in Angel and Islington would turn into 10 years of friendship, love, and adventure. Thank you for every moment of it, I would not have come this far without you by my side.